All Pov to the Imagination!

Revolutionary class struggle in trade unions and the petty bourgeois fetish of organisational purity

Dave Douglass

Published by The Class War Federation
PO Box 467, London E8 3QX
© 1999 David Douglass
ISBN 0 95373470 6
British Library Cataloguing-in-Publication Data:
A catalogue record for this book is available from the British Library
First edition October 1999
Printed by Top Printers Ltd, London NW10 0RG

Dedication

This pamphlet is dedicated to my Da, John, who died while it was in the process of being written. The son of a miner and later father of a miner he had been born into a baptism of fire as a young pitlad in the 1926 strike, struggling to support the rest of the family because his Da was laid up owing to the noxious fumes of the mines. Greatly inspired by the British Wobbly and De Leonist, Lodge Secretary George Harvey, he joined pickets and mass meetings and lobbies, was charged by sabre wielding cavalry, and dispersed from the Newcastle city streets by bayonet fixed marines. He scrabbled for coal, walked miles for food, gathered berries and weeds to eat and nie starved to death. His religion was the democracy and passion of the primitive Methodists without fine robes and big cathedrals, his principles built on granite. Despite a lifetime in crucifying underground conditions he refused to drink, smoke or swear. He dedicated himself to the Labour Party especially after the war when he felt it had taken steps to resolve grave social injustices. By the time of Wilson's big, though impotent majority, he grew disillusioned, & as Kinnock turned his venom on the miners and cheer-led the state's forces against the miners once again, he felt utter betrayal and resolved never to work for that party again, something he had tirelessly done hitherto. He was an avid reader of working class literature, a fine tenor in the male voice choir, unsuppressable comic and inexhaustible walker. He is an irreplaceable tutor.

We argued all the time, about history, meanings of life, the class struggle and class organisation. This pamphlet is within **that** tradition.

John Douglass

Born 6th April 1908 -- Jarrow Colliery
Died 27 May 1995 -- Wardley Colliery.

About The Author

Certain comrades, confounded by a strong challenge to what is in my view their petty bourgeois caricature of struggle in "trade unions" and wrong footed from my designation as a Coal Miner, have incredibly sought to refute the former by way of discrediting the latter. Some of this comes down to pig ignorance of the structures of the Unions in general and the NUM in particular. Echanges Et Mouvement, chiding Class War for an uncensored feature article of mine in Heavy Stuff 5 ask:- "..the signature of David Douglass "Yorkshire Miner" (can we consider a NUM Branch Delegate as a miner?)[1]. Wildcat takes this a little further: "we should point out that he (i.e. David Douglass) was not just expressing his opinion but defending his role in society. He is not, as he likes to describe himself, a "Yorkshire Miner" but a full time NUM delegate." Then, as frequently happens on the left, this "information" is repeated by other organisations until a totally inaccurate piece of information becomes a well known matter of fact. Anarchist Communist Federation published it in Organise, throwing in the new revelation, my Full Time Union Position as "Vice Chair" of South Yorkshire NUM Panel. Class War internal Education Bulletin republished the Wildcat article, but unilaterally, and without either permission of the authors or knowledge of their readers, altered and corrected the misinformation! A bit like withdrawing the charge but leaving you on trial.

The true situation (which is so easy to discover if you wanted to put across an accurate picture)[2] is that for 29 years I have been a coal miner in the coalfields of Durham and South Yorkshire. Since 1979 I have been the elected NUM Branch Delegate for Hatfield Colliery. NUM Delegates must be miners themselves, not just at the time of the election but during their term of office. The delegate (and all the other branch officials, with the exception of some Secretaries at the time, although now they too work underground) continue to do their own jobs, in my case on the coal face as a "Ripper" and on the crippling shift cycle of Days, Aft's, Evenings, and Nights. The delegates, when on Union duty representing the men or their families before appeals and tribunals, inquests or whatever, receive somewhat less than the average wage of the workers, can be removed from office at any time by a mass vote of no confidence, and face bi-annual ballot box election. The South Yorkshire NUM Panel is a non paid, voluntary position in what is anyway an unofficial assembly of local Branches aimed at checking Executive powers. I have also been briefly a member of the NUM Area Executive during the period of growing militancy up to and through the duration of the great strike when the members in combative spirits elected far left candidates from the Doncaster coalfield. The Area EC usually meets once every two months, and if you're successful in gaining time off work, you receive the union's day's wage, (about 25% less of the day's earnings one would receive at work). The position likewise in no way saves you from the bad back or pulled knackers on the night shift, and neither should it. Despite "Analysis's" proposition that the NUM is "... the most bureaucratic organisation in the world", the NUM nationally, at the time

1) Echanges Et Mouvement
2) After all, members of "Wildcat", for example, were obviously present at the International Class War Conference at which I was speaking. If that cat is so wild, how come it didn't jump on the stage and confront me face to face with the accusations they later formulated when I was 250 miles away, and in a publication so obscure, it was years before I got to see it. Wildcat? I doubt they would make a decent puddy tat.

the critics were writing, had only TWO (2) full time officers. Today it has only one, whilst the Yorkshire Area of the NUM, with more than half the total mining workforce in Britain, also only has one full time official. I am neither of these, nor have I ever been, and since I have now been blacklisted and victimised for the last 5 years I am unlikely ever to become so. I have however always been a coalminer suffering the self same deprivations and conditions as the men who have chosen me to represent them. This is a privilege I am honoured to have had.[3]

I will argue in this pamphlet, as I have in a number of others, that the Miners, in a succession of Unions over the last two hundred years, and more informally for a hundred years before that, have frequently played a revolutionary role and aspired to revolutionary ideology and action; that the NUM, warts and all, had far more genuine working class credentials than any of its self proclaimed revolutionary critics. It follows from this that I am not "Heavily Implicated" in the NUM, as the ACF puts it, but heavily *involved* in its struggles for social justice for the mining communities and the working class in general. I have never drawn more than my loss of earnings and travelling expenses in service of that Union, but had I become a paid employee of the Union I should not have found this in any way contradictory to my Communist principles and values.

Politically a revolutionary Marxist on the Anarchist left, member of South Yorkshire Class War, and the IWW. In the recent Class War split over dissolution or continuation I have stuck with The Class War Federation continuation. Likewise I have found work in the Northern Anarchist Network useful and enjoyable. I have written in the past a regular column in the (reformed) CPGB paper Weekly Worker, at their non sectarian invitation to supply the paper and its widespread readership in the left and Trade Union Movement with an update on politics and industrial and social developments in the coalfields and the NUM. This has made me the jibe of titles like "Anarcho-Stalinist" etc. My views on political vanguards and Parties will be made clear in this publication but I make no apology for utilising the platform they offered me without compromise of either my own or their (different) political positions, but this is perhaps old news since the coalfields no longer occupy their former central place in the labour movement, and my column has withered along with them and is unlikely to be revived. It might be added incidentally that Class War itself is printed on the CPGB press without any compromise to *its* political integrity.

---

3) It should also be said for fear of another "revelation" that I have had spells of full time and part time education, always remaining an NUM member: working holidays - back at the colliery, and always back on the coal face, and always going back underground after graduation. This is a tradition among coal communities, regarding education as a benefit to be used for the good of the working class rather than an escape ladder out of it.

Introduction

The origins of this particular polemic are varied, and now lay some distance in the recent past, beginning with my furious response to Comrade Brendel's <u>Autonomous Class Struggle In Britain 1945-1980</u>[4] in <u>Some Thoughts As I Read The Pamphlet "Autonomous Class Struggle in Great Britain"</u>. I gave it a mention in my general analysis of the role of the left during the Miners Strike of '84-85 in my address to the International Conference of Class War under the title <u>Refracted Perspective</u>, later republished in Heavy Stuff under the title Charge Of The Left Brigade. Unbeknown to me a fierce reply was made by Brendel and backed up by Theo Sander in Goodbye To The Unions published by Echanges et Mouvement. I only got to see this publication relatively recently. Into the middle of all this came the last great pit closure plan and the miners, myself included, took the national offensive in an effort to halt the government in their tracks and mobilise enough widespread opposition not only to stop the closures but shake the Tories from office. It was a fight to save OUR UNION (this translates in pit communities as ourselves, our lives, our dignity, our sense of self respect, our families, our futures, our pasts, what we aspire to) by saving the mines.

I was born into the Tyneside of shipyard, heavy engineering, railways and pits. This was a region in which the Union was its heart, in the pit communities of Britain the Union has been its soul as well. The Union was our ability to intervene into life and society to challenge things, to stand up for ourselves. Whether a corner of a field in far off Barnsley had a pit in it or not was not the fundamental issue, it never was just jobs. So with this in mind we come to London, with our banners and bands and our kids, and our retired folk, and are met by a bunch of people giving out leaflets saying they were AGAINST THE UNIONS! We had never ever come across "Anti Unionism" on our side of the class divide. It was the Anarchist Communist Federation, and they drew another furious polemic with me in the pages of Organise.

Since then WILDCAT published a vitriolic attack upon me ("OUTSIDE AND AGAINST THE UNIONS") and my central proposition while SUBVERSION and one or two other individuals with word processors adopting organisational names cheer-led the anti unionists from the sidelines. Reviews of our various contributions have been carried right across Europe and in

---

4) Autonomous Class Struggle In Britain 1945-1980 Cajo Brendel, although actually I was responding to an edited partially re-written version of it, which I was unaware of at the time. I had assumed Cajo must be a situationist, since his arguments (to me anyway) sounded similar. I was wrong, and I unreservedly apologise for having offended his political lineage. He turns out to be a veteran Council Communist, an ideology I had hitherto never come across. Arial writing in Spartacus enlightens us:- "... has led some to reject any form of union organisation altogether. In most particular the council communists movement... Council communist theory long ago forced all "pure" council communist organisations to disappear up their own arse in a cloud of logic. Because they place their bets entirely on the spontaneous creation of workers' councils in times of crisis and view all organisations - unions or parties - as inherently reactionary, there own organisations are therefore cancelled out by their own theory.

most of the Libertarian and revolutionary Marxist press, and we have made it the centre of many conferences and educational schools. Incredibly Wildcat and Organise say the point of my intervention is to "Stifle criticism of the unions".

Flicked in the raw by my assertion that workers in their own class struggle organisations, official and unofficial, are more revolutionary than the outside organisations attempting to lead them. That the vanguard parties and vanguard perspectives are unwelcome. ACF calls me "A Bureaucrat heavily implicated in the NUM". Wildcat calls me "An Anarcho Leninist", poisonous Analysis "An Anarcho-Stalinist Rent A Gob". Sometimes they've also been personal. I try not to sink too far into this level of abuse in my responses but have allowed myself some angry indulgence.

I consider that many of these groups have only a vague concept of the nature of working people's lives. Yet still they have determined a role which they consider we have to play. After all, whereas I am forced to present this CV of my background and life in response to the distortions mentioned, your average Mr and Ms Organisational purer than thou critic need only don a Donkey jacket and join some fiery sounding anarchist group to be absorbed into "the working class" despite the very finest of upper class backgrounds and most cosseted of lifestyles. Wildcat declare that they are the working class, and as such everything they think, publish or do is of course the actions of the working class; no need to get down to actually finding out where the mass of people are, or how they see the struggle, just cobble your own reality together and you've cracked it. We have seen this a thousand times: whatever the occupants of the hall of mirrors which is "The Revolutionary Party" do, this is the action of the risen revolutionary working class. Photo of six people in woolly hats and combat jackets with hand painted signs, caption: "Masses demand build the Workers Revolutionary Party Now".

Such groups relate to workers as a nebulous vacuous entity, a blank sheet, or aimless crowd. They don't like us when we present our own ideas directly, or challenge the stereotypes of class struggle and organisation which they have patiently worked out for us. These differences are not simply POLITICAL and POLEMICAL but basically CLASS antagonisms. It puts me in mind of something someone said in the 1930s about "Communists who can't stand the stink of the Proletariat."

All Power to the Imagination!

Class Struggle in Unions

In the unlikely event that a coal miner born on generations of mining should chance in conversation on the subject of "Unions" with an academic skilled in industrial relations or business studies, the conversation would rapidly run aground. The two would find an imme- diate mutually exclusive language barrier. I am not here talking of the ancient dialects of Northumbria or Wales against that of the Oxbridge grammarian English, but the conceptual understanding of "Unions" and trade unionism.

The miner would at once regard "the union" as being him and his marra's[5]; the union's history as his history, from cradle to grave, that of his parents, grandparents and much of the region of his residence also. The Union marks the pages of his personal and class history, the conditions of his current working life against that of his father and grandfather, the terms that govern his hours of labour, his wages, the age of his marras, even their sex, is established in epochs of union struggle, class struggle remembered and learned. Governments. Prime Min- isters, are seen in relation to the Union's contact with them and their mutual responses to one another. Baldwin? 1926 General Strike. Churchill? Murderer of the miners - ruling class warrior. Heath? Two to us. Thatcher? Most deadly of enemies, etc. Like kings and queens in bour- geois history, time itself is marked out in epochs of struggle, open or covert, official or unofficial, Labourite or Revolutionary dominated, but the Union, like the coal seam itself, runs through the life and death of the communities, from benefit funds and convalescent homes at birth to death grants and inquest advocacy and widow protection, or as Mick McGahey put it, "From the erection to the resurrection.

Does our Oxbridge professor see 'The Union" in such a light? No, when he talks of "The Union" he means formal organisational structures, he means organisational models, the lead- ers, the rulebook the balance sheets, the office blocks. When he looks at conflict he looks at "dysfunction", at conciliation, arbitration processes, the letter and legal meaning of agree- ments etc.

So does society receive a composite of both these images? No, it is the image that the media makes out for "unions" and the preconceived notion of what unions are for which is passed on from bourgeois and petty bourgeois commentators and academics. It is this image, rather than that seen by the miners and their families which much of left themselves take on board. Not themselves involved with the world of work and industry and collective organisation and

---

5) Marra = workmate

cultures, it is the formal bricks and mortar model of Unions which they will consider. Sometimes the left will have academic models of their own put forward by middle class revolutionaries such as Lenin or Trotsky. These will take formal union functions, such as the wage bargaining, or the well heeled Union Leader and sellout, and draft this into an organisational proscription carved in stone. As Workers Solidarity Movement puts it: "This can lead revolutionaries to conclude that the unions are now part of the state machine, just one more means of controlling workers. This has manifest itself in other countries in the view that workers should leave the unions and destroy them; that no permanent organisation of workers under capitalism can avoid becoming totally integrated into the state and a tool in the hands of the bosses.

The people who promote this claim argue that the unions are holding workers back from making revolution... now! We are very easy on them when we dismiss their position as childish and ultra-leftist. But the point about becoming part of the state machine does appear to have some basis, especially when you take into account the Programme for Economic and Social Progress based upon "social partnership" between employers, government and unions. To make this case it is argued that there is no essential difference between the bureaucracy and the union as a whole. Clearly it is a nonsense to describe the majority of workers as part of the state machine.[6]

Having made the organisation a monolith, its role will be henceforth preordained. It will function in only one way, it can be seen in only one way, it works in only one way, "this is what Unions are". Much of the petty bourgeois anarchist movement comes along and wishes to view "Unions". It takes up the ready made models and bases its views upon these rather than a conflicting reality. Where struggle is clearly happening in the workplace and across industry, this can be explained by the fine tortuous adjustment such as that developed by my old sparring partner Cajo Brendel. The class struggle is "autonomous" and "anti the Unions"; the betrayal, compromise and anti working class behaviour *is* Trade Unionism. Even when actually, in every case, the struggles Cajo is so delighted with are taking place in UNIONS, albeit at lower levels or unofficially. Even when the activists he cites are Trade Unionists, sometimes Shop Stewards, Branch Officials or whatever.

Take a youngster from a pit community with generations of mining relations, going up to university, and perhaps because of her background taking in a history of the coal industry, hoping to find something of her parents' and grandparents' past. Instead she is given a list of bourgeois historians, economic historians, "Labour/industrial relations" commentators. Perhaps a left wing tutor has tried to redress the balance by suggesting Page Arnot. With Arnot she would find a more sympathetic view of the Union side of things, but the "Union" here, as in the other cases, will be the arbitration deals, details of who sat where, price lists and tables, etc. Pick up his famous "The Miners" and search its pages for *the miners,* for the bloke at the pick point, for the aspirations of his family and community, for the women folk, she will look hard and find little.[7] None of these commentators see the underline essence of what

---

6) Anarchism and The Unions, Dublin May 6th 1992.
7) A partial exception has been Huw Benyon and Terry Austrin's recent book Masters and Servants, Class

unions are, their human components. They only see the formal structure related to the philo-
sophically predetermined model. This is why anyone setting off from the proposition *"What
is our attitude to Trade Unions?"* rather than *"What is our attitude to workers in struggle?"*
will, invariably, get the answer wrong. To view the issue this way lends itself to an analysis
not of the working class, which is the union in reality, and its body and soul of aspirations,
but instead of grey empty structures, leading to arguments about hierarchies, bought off
bureaucrats and the views of functionaries.

In truth the only way working class students can avoid regurgitating bourgeois value systems is to get down and research the questions first hand, reflecting the lives, the memories
and meanings ordinary people themselves put upon things, maybe adding a few pages to
working people's own history directly. The work of the History Workshop and the countless
little histories and accounts written by thousands of women and sometimes children about
the events of '84-85 and the traumas since bear strong testimony to this.

Arial's review <u>Socialism and Trade Unions</u> does not go far enough in their conclusions, but
I agree wholeheartedly "they" (the Communist Workers Organisation, but it applies to a
number of such groups) "make this mistake because they discuss trade unions at such a high
level of abstraction, forgetting that the essence of the trade union is workers uniting to
protect their interests in the workplace, and that ultimately the union and the workers of
whom it consists are one and the same thing. If these workers have a reformist outlook on life,
i.e. believe that capitalism can be made to run in the interests of all, the unions must have the
same outlook; on the other hand if there were more revolutionary workers in the unions and
in society in general - then the unions would have a more revolutionary outlook no longer
harbouring any illusions about "common national interest" or other such rubbish.

That would not in any way alter the essential nature and role of unions as the defensive
organisations of the working class; but it would make them far more effective in fulfilling that
role.[8] This is a little overstated. Unions are of course never wholly reformist or radical or
revolutionary, often there is fierce class war, at least in an ideological and organisational
sense, being fought out within the union. These are struggles about different perceptions of
the world, and whether to, and how to change it. Some unions do have more or less more
radical or conservative cultures reflecting those workers' social histories, the type of work,
area etc. they inhabit. "Anti Union" sees no distinctions; revolutionary to Labour Party
councillor, the whole class as it struggles for political perceptions is dismissed at least in so
far as they comprise the Unions. Neither can it be said "unions" are a homogeneous body.
There are, at the factory floor and pick point, workers far more militant and combative than in
the presidential office of the Union's Head Quarters. The role of the union bureaucrat is
legion and I shall return to it, but this parasitic phenomenon cannot be allowed to characterise "Unions" *per se.*

---

and Patronage In the Making of a Labour Organisation, Rivers Oram Press, London, 1994. Although
spellbound and delighted by the workings and grandeur of the Durham miners bureaucracy, the book contains
fascinating insights and anecdotal chapters on the miners, their wives and communities.
8)Article in Spartacus, organising bulletin for Socialists in Norfolk and Suffolk.,Oct. 94

"Trade union strugle is a necessity for two reasons. Firstly to protect and improve conditions - if unions disappeared tomorrow, does anyone think the bosses would not go on all-out offensive against workers? Just look at conditions in countries where genuine unions are suppressed, like Taiwan, Indonesia or Thailand, with child labour, starvation wages, and violent repression of dissent on the shopfloor. Secondly, as Anarchists we recognise that when workers are brought into struggle they can develop a sense of their collective power and become more open to radical ideas. A good example is the Gateaux strike a couple of years ago. This group of workers had not had a strike for as long as anyone could remember. They certainly were not considered the shock troops of Dublin trade unionism. Yet within days they were illegally occupying the workplace, asking left groups including the WSM to join a support committee, and sending flying pickets to try to picket out the workers in their sister company, Allied Lyons in Drimnagh."[9]

At the end of '94 myself and the other members of Doncaster and Sheffield Class War were invited to a public debate with what was to us an odd ball group (yes, *more* odd ball than us!) - The Communist Workers Organisation. Turns out many were ex members of the diseased and deceased Anarchist Workers Group, same as the so called "Analysis" person (Small world, isn't it?). They chose the title **Are Trade Unions Revolutionary?** and in a sentence even before we had started the debate, they had managed to encapsulate how entirely they miss the point.

Trade Unions, in the terms they look at them, are basically *inanimate* objects and therefore cannot make revolution. IT IS THE WORKING CLASS, AS A CLASS, WHICH IS REVOLUTIONARY, AND WHO WILL MAKE REVOLUTION. What I argue is that workers can utilise their own class instruments to do this. Initially, yes, in the union form, but at which point it has already begun to be transformed from say the simple Leninist model of what a Trade Union is.

Are buses revolutionary? Of course not, but why not? Because buses are inanimate objects. What if a bus is seized to charge a police cordon, or is overturned and set on fire to stop blacklegs or the fascists; what if one is packed with dynamite and left in "The Golden Mile2 outside the Stock Exchange? Is this a bus being used for revolutionary purposes? Of course it is. Was it designed for such a purpose, is its structure capable of standing these extraordinary purposes? Doubtful. So what *transformed* the bus from a simple inanimate object to a revolutionary instrument for which it clearly wasn't designed?

The conscious intervention of oppressed human beings, that's all.[10] I remember an American newsreel film during the Vietnam war taken from inside a US gunship, and the pilot is report-

---

9) Anarchism and The Trade Unions, Dublin, May 6th 1992.
10) During the '84-85 miners strike we grabbed everything to hand to use as weapons, one of the more inventive of which was at Silverwood Colliery when a motorised lawn mower (!) was broken from its Council Works shed, and used to head up the charge against numerous riot police. Although the vehicle had a seat only for one on this occasion it carried a full compliment of several missile throwing miners and proved quite unstoppable as it careered in one direction after another. A moment of glory even in the life of an unsuspecting grass cutter.

ing, "Have sighted five Vietcong *and a Vietcong horse.*" So if the bus, and the horse, can be instruments of the revolution when oppressed people utilise them with that conscious design, I fail to see why a Union, in times of class conflict of sufficient scale, cannot also be so utilised. As demonstrably it has already been so, particularly my own union.[11] At the risk of sounding repetitive, is there anybody still who does not know why the miners were subject to an outright war of liquidation by all branches of the State, including MI5, the Army, the DSS, The Police, the Cabinet, The Stock Exchange, The National Media, etc. etc? This was a plan to destroy the miners and their union, The NUM, which the state saw as a political, class threat *in potentially revolutionary terms.*[12]

However there is a sense in which the term *The Union* is a misnomer, since this suggests a unitary object, whereas it is at all times composed of conflicting tendencies. It is, though, simply inaccurate, not to say dishonest, to portray 'the Miners' for example to be in conflict with 'the Union' unless one qualifies this as meaning perhaps Union Leaders as against pit lodges *of the union*. After a lifetime in the coal industry I can think of not a single example where these conflicting forces of ideology, or position, were not reflected in one aspect of "the union" over another. My recent book Pit Sense Versus The State[13] relates to this little told aspect of the great coal strike of '84. The struggle between pit branches and the leadership, between the Area leadership and the National, between moderate areas and militant, between strikers and scabs, between reluctant strikers and activists, all of which are reflected in the union. Given this context can it now clearly be seen how a proposition of "Anti The Union" becomes literally a nonsense, totally negative and unable to relate to any of the trends or conflicts as they are actually occurring?

It seems a simple point to me: people and people's consciousness, their ability to intervene, the strength of that intervention, will determine whether the union is a union so perceived by the outside caricature, whether the bus will continue its humdrum drive through suburbia, whether the horse remains a nonentity of history, or all become instruments of insurrection.

My friends in the CPGB told me recently in response to a critical letter of mine in Daily Worker, that the miners could only develop "Trade Union Consciousness" in the NUM. To fight for socialism you had to belong to a different "quality" of organisation, in their case the Commu-

---

11) See, Coal Communities In Conflict, published by Class War. Or The Miners Association, a Trade Union in the Age of the Chartists. By R Challiner.

12) Of course this is a dynamic process, not a static one. The NUM bureaucracy and that of the MFGB before it at times fought pitched battles with the rank and file miners in their independent Lodges or alliances of lodges. It is also true that some of our leaders had been more radical than the membership who at times left the field of battle, leaving such men utterly destitute and blacklisted to die and be buried in abject poverty. Likewise the conflicting cultural and political and religious identities *between* bodies and areas of miners have pushed and pulled the union organisation in one direction or another. But this is always done as part of the union as such. The occupants of the Red Villages on Tyneside and Durham who in the nineteenth century fought bitter battles with some of the leaders of the union bureaucracy all regarded themselves as *union men* whilst so too the leaders battled for control over *the union*. This is in microcosm the pattern of the class war as a whole. A process of conflicting and contesting forces within the class as well as outwith the class. Its is not a single readymade event. See The Durham Miners, in Miners, Quarrymen and Saltworkers, published Routledge and Keegan Paul, Ed, Ralph Samuels.

13) Pit Sense Versus The State, A History of Militant Doncaster Miners, pub Phoenix Press.

nist Party, though of course the other Vanguardists would substitute their own name, for the "quality" organisation.

This mystical transformation theory always reminds me of those primitive tribal ceremonies where the young lad enters the dark cave, and has spiders and bugs run all over him before emerging *"no longer a boy, but a man!"* The cave has transformed the human being in a magical and mystical way. So it is that the worker lives his subliminal life unable to see above the horizons of more wages until they are led to the distant light of the special organisation, whereupon they are transformed to full consciousness.

Why is this? Surely the worker can perceive just as well in one organisation as another? For it is Perception, and Consciousness which determine the level of thought and understanding, not the badge on the lapel or a special handshake or some mystical magical organisation. COMRADES, THERE REALLY IS NOTHING IN THE CAVE.

We must recognise that workers in class struggle are engaged in a war across a whole frontier of differing conflicts, in the school, on the streets, at work, on the dole, with the Council or the landlord, in the community, in race, gender, age and sexual issues. The class conflict manifests itself in a variety of ways and through a number of forms; in the case in point, the struggle in the workplace generally takes place in Unions. This is simply a fact. The union is seen by workers as an instrument in their fight for social survival. It is both absurd and reactionary to petulantly stand, face to the wall, saying "I'm agin the Unions" in some purer than thou stance, while millions upon millions of workers utilise them as frontline weapons of the class war.

In any case, we must not allow ourselves to fall into the trap of departmentalising what is a general process, and not a specific one. Revolutionary consciousness and revolutionary challenges take place across society, one stimulating the other. They are not confined to some exclusive unitary element, neither are they constrained by specific forms.

In the late '60s what could be called a general revolutionary current spread out from 3rd world struggles, out through college and university, out through oppressed races, for gender and sexual liberation, to pits, and docks from factory to art, design, theatre, film making, poetry, rock music. It challenged yes, in workplace occupations, in the rise of the unofficial workers' movement in the mines, in the wildcat loose in the car factory and docks, but simultaneously it did so in the free festival, in the politics of sexual freedom, of the psychedelic sub-culture as well as anti-imperialism. It was a symbiotic process.

Does anyone think we as young miners were going to be confined to some grey constraints of something called "The Trade Union Movement" while half the generation was rocking the night away and shagging all over the place? We were into that! The best slogan of the period summarised the fundamental demand linking all:-

ALL POWER TO THE IMAGINATION!! The workers' struggle was part of a general world-wide revolutionary movement, perception and "something" that was in the air. Industrial organisation, all right, but our imaginations demanded power also. We did not feel the singularity that goes with doctrines of "the one true road"; there were many roads, marching separately but striking together, as we would have put it. As young white working class revolutionary workers, we thought of the Panthers for example as *our* party in America, they were the people on the ground fighting an aspect of the war which was inextricably linked to our own. When at our invitation they spoke to mass meetings in the Miners Welfares in the Doncaster coalfield, young white pitlads hung on their every word, seeing in them role models, comrades, fellow workers or just plain "dead cool dudes". When the Provos emerged kicking and shooting out of the republican ghettos of occupied Ulster we didn't need to have them go through a telephone directory or checklist of politically correct question and answers to recognise fellow young workers fighting, guns in hand, against loyalist bigot, southern bourgeois and an imperialist army before we recognised where that piece of the world revolutionary process fitted in or which side of the class line we stood on. We didn't all have to fight in the same way, in the same form of organisation to be on the same side in the same war. We aren't all oppressed in exactly the same way. Different situations, different periods, different cultures and experiences throw up different organisational forms of struggle.

Comrade Bobby Sands, in his poem The Rhythm Of Time, written whilst 'on the blanket' protest, against the attempt by first the Labour Government and then the Tories to criminalise the Republican activists by withdrawal of Political Status, and for which he sacrificed his fine young life, encapsulates the way many young workers of our generation interconnected struggles …

There's an inner thing in every man,
Do you know this thing my friend?
It has withstood the blows of a million years
And will do so to the end.

It was born when time did not exist
And it grew up out of life
It cut down evil's strangling vines,
Like a slashing searing knife.

It lit fires when fires were not
and burnt the mind of man,
Tempering leadened hearts to steel
From the time that time began.

It went by the waters of Babylon,
And when all men were a loss,
It screeched in writhing agony,
And it hung bleeding from the cross.

It died in Rome by lion and sword
And in defiant cruel array,
When the deathly word was Spartacus
Along the Appian Way.

It marched with Wat the Tyler's poor,
And frightened lord and king,
And it was emblazoned in their deathly stare
As e'er a living thing.

It smiled in holy innocence
Before conquistadors of old,
So meek and tame and unaware,
Of the deathly power of gold.

It burst forth through pitiful Paris streets,
And stormed the old Bastille
And marched upon the serpent's head,
And crushed it 'neath its heel.

It died in blood on Buffalo Plains,
and starved by moons of rain,
Its heart was buried in Wounded Knee,
But it will come to rise again.

It screamed aloud by Kerry lakes,
As it was knelt upon the ground
And it died in great defiance,
As they coldly shot it down.

It is found in every light of hope,
It knows no bounds nor space,
It has risen in red and black and white,
It is there in every race.

It lies in the hearts of heroes dead,
It screams in tyrants' eyes,
It has reached the peak of mountains high,
It comes searing 'cross the skies.

It lights the dark of this prison cell,
It thunders forth its might,
It is 'the undauntable thought' my friend,
That thought that says "I'm right".

We must not allow the 'party builders' or vanguardist elitist Anarcho sect, who reify their own institutions and perceptions and see everything in such institutional ways, to obscure the conscious intervention of people attempting to shape their own destinies despite organisational and institutional limitations.

There does come a time, when frontline defence organisations are pushed to the limit of their usefulness and run into the obstacle of their internal limitations and political contradictions. The fact that such an event is foreseeable by wise armchair theorists many miles from the battle in no way should urge us to get out of the ranks of the march and onto the cynical sidewalk. Just the contrary. Supporting the mass struggle of the people, supporting its most militant wing, and fighting for our own political viewpoint as we go, is an act of class solidarity and not just a political manoeuvre. It stands us, in the times of contradiction and crisis, alongside our comrades and fellow workers and in the forefront of the debate, having engaged blow for blow in the struggle this far. This applies in the workers' industrial struggle, in a very practical sense on the shop floor and the office and school, but also elsewhere, as In Ireland, Palestine or South Africa.

The fight against anti-Semitic ethnic cleansing, land theft and Zionist imperialism by the Palestinian peoples has, until comparatively recent times, found its political expression within the broad, socialistic, secular PLO. The masses engaged in armed struggle, and the civilian populace of the beleaguered villages fighting with rocks against armoured trucks, centralised around one or other of the factions covered by the term PLO. Of course Anarchists could abstain from the whole debate on the basis of the less than pure programme, or the bourgeois leadership, or 'nationalism' and instead dream up a perfect solution, one which no doubt would drop from heaven and not arise from the actual struggle the people were engaged in. If we are genuine about internationalism, about knowing our fight when we see it, whatever its form, about knowing the contents of working and exploited peoples' hearts and what at base they are really fighting for, we cannot take such an abstentionist view. The situation now, however, is one where the limitations of Arafat and his ever more compromist position has brought home the contradictions. Palestinian police shoot down stonethrowers and worshippers, just like the Zionists did. The collapse of the socialist/communist wing of the secular movement into a liberal tailing of the petty bourgeois pro-capitalist wing and their subsequent selling out of the struggle, has given rise to growing religious fundamentalism and medievalism behind the mullahs and Hezbollah, posing a worse situation for working class non-Zionist Jews in Israel and working class Arabs, particularly the women, alike. The sparse areas of water-starved desert & totally reliant territories conceded to the new Palestinian state must leave a bitter taste in the mouths of those driven from the fertile plains and self supporting areas under Zionist occupation.

The new state will soon confront the Palestinian working class as such and pose directly *class against class* within the exploited nationality. The much vaunted "Peace Agreement" of Oct. 98 seals many fates, not least that of PLO officialdom. Everywhere they are utterly discredited, as traitors and corrupt bureaucrats lording over the so called freed areas. Secondly it seals the fate of a negotiated principled settlement, incorporating an end of the occupation and colonisation, a return of the refugees, and the recognition of Arab East Jerusalem as the capital of an independent Palestinian territory. The current agreement makes it quite plain nothing of that will be forthcoming.

Proud Arabs and Texan Oilmen

Finally it seals the fate of Gaza. The so called 13% extra land given over to Palestinian control is marginally WORSE off than it was before the agreement. 3% of that 13 is under "joint"

Israeli/Palestinian military control (ie it is under Israeli control), it separates the strip into three surrounded and disjointed, unviable areas. For the million impoverished and increasingly hopeless Palestinian refugees in Gaza, facing 4,000 arrogant, deeply racialist, often rich and opulent settlers protected by machine gun posts and tanks, this is a tinderbox growing ever more volatile by the day. When the explosion happens it will be desperate and outside the control of Fatah, increasingly seen as compromist and useless. Such an explosion is likely to see carnage reaped upon the whole colonial settlement without mercy or discretion, and heavily out-gunned and vulnerable, a massacre by the Zionist state which could follow could well itself mark a rising spiral involving many of the neighbouring Arab and Muslim countries, and Europe too. Currently the only resistance is led by sectarian and fundamentalist Hamas and Jihad, although the bulk of the Palestinian people have not yet abandoned their communistic and secular vision of themselves as part of a world struggle by the poor and dispossessed against capitalism and imperialism. How such sentiments will be organised and orientated is unclear at present, amid the growing despair. But we can say from out of these contradictory situations a genuine revolutionary libertarian, secular campaign can arise, but it will arise from the mass of the people previously on the street and roughly associated with the title PLO, if only very tenuously.

This same could be seen in South Africa with the ANC and in Ireland with Sinn Fein. With the former, the mass of industrial workers are taking COSATU away from its cosy relationship with the ANC leadership and demanding that it fight for wages and conditions now, irrespective of what colour the face is in the president's chair or on the Board of Directors. The South African Communist Party will most assuredly split along class lines with members close to the people breaking from its collaborationist direction and in support of independent working class action, whilst others will see a social democratic future in a multi-racial capitalist South Africa. With the latter (Ireland) unions have long been a totally irrelevant feature of life in occupied Ulster. The Unions, like most of the work, being totally subservient to Loyalism and in support of British occupation. The impasse of the peace process had allowed the debate to shift for a time away from the politics of the last bullet fired and into wider areas of organisation. New class-for-itself movements seemed to be beginning to arise with less traditional "nationalist" orientation, the prisoners in particular leading the van toward a clearer *class* orientation, whilst the ceasefire allowed a little more radical and socialistic thought to emerge in the "loyalist" community. All of this demonstrates that centres around which struggles genuinely focus are always in the process of flux, and new movements and tendencies arise almost inevitably as the organisation hits the changing objective forces and range of demands and levels of class consciousness as they inter-relate. Bold though the peace initiative was in putting Major and the British state under the world spotlight and gaining 'respectable' political status for Sinn Fein for the first time since it kicked its way out of the ghettos, it didn't take the UK state long to probe the weaknesses and retake the initiative. Calling off the armed struggle would only ever work if the state was prepared to make serious concessions in return. With Major a prisoner to the Loyalist MPs and with Blair's New labour stuck right up his political backside, there was no imperative to do so. Indeed intelligence suggested that, having called off the relentless guerrilla war, the community were relaxing for the first time in a generation & it would be a risky business cranking it up again with less than wholehearted support. That being the case, having nailed Sinn Fein's colours to the "Democratic and Peaceful process" mast a complete U turn back behind the guerrillas was going to be very difficult without major splits and disarray between tendencies in the military and political sections, whatever the UK State did or didn't do. So why do anything? Sinn Fein was perhaps naive in underestimating the cynicism of its old adversary or its willingness to risk the explosive fury of the IRA getting its thing going again. The bomb at Canary Wharf and anything similar was small beer in return for having split and to some extent *subverted* the revolutionary republican movement. With the Peace Process back on board, Sinn Fein are faced daily with the fact of a *de facto* Loyalist veto on any softly softly backdoor into a 32 county Ireland. Something less than the principle of an all island of Ireland is being assimilated and we have seen the first major breaks in '97-98 of senior IRA Council members, and the formation of The 32 County Committee, a provisional's Provos in embryo led significantly by Bobby Sands' sister and posing a militant break from the swamp of compromise which Adams and the current leadership are drowning slowly into. The greatest impetus the peace process has enjoyed was the Real IRA bombing of Omagh.

We will take no lectures from the 'bomber' British state on morality and innocent victims. This is the state which was quite happy to target civilians in Germany during world war two, making a point of blitzing cities with no military or strategic importance, in a purely terrorist rationale. The flooding of the Rhur during the dambuster raids was aimed at killing non-combatant civilians, particularly coalminers, factory workers and of course women and tens of thousands of children. Britain excused these massacres because they were to further its political and military aims. The fact that the kids at Dresden didn't know who Hitler was or that the town simply manufactured crockery didn't matter a bugger to the generals, they were to be blown away in a massive fire storm following blanket bombing. Of course Britain applauded the dropping of nuclear bombs on two civilian Japanese cities, Hiroshima and Nagasaki, again cities with absolutely no military purpose and containing only civilian non-combatant men, women and children. The planes having been sent over at the same time on three successive days so people wouldn't fear them and wouldn't be in shelters, thus causing the maximum possible loss of life to the civilians. Of course they also knew two weeks in advance that Coventry was to be subject to a mass air raid by the Germans, but didn't want them to know of its spying techniques and deliberately allowed the city to be bombed without evacuation so as not to alert them. This was as good as bombing Coventry and 'their own' people themselves.

Then there is Britain's infamous "first nuclear strike" policy. Whilst the USSR and the USA said they would only use nuclear weapons if attacked with nuclear weapons, the British state openly pledged to use them first, incinerating whole Soviet cities full men, women and children with nuclear weapons if they were losing a conventional war in Europe. The mass bombing of Iraq in more recent times killed civilians, children included, and refugees, all in the name of furthering Britain's political and military aims in the area. In the same week as the Omagh bombing, the biggest terrorist organisation in the world, The USA, unleashed 70 cruise missiles on two third world countries, Afghanistan and Sudan. In no-warning attacks they struck without the slightest regard for loss of life to innocent men, women and children, bombing a medical factory in Sudan in a nonsensical and totally invented claim that it made germ warfare components. Blair was the first in the world to congratulate the bombers while weeping crocodile tears for innocents in Omagh and pontificating about the immorality of men who pursue political aims by violent methods. In April '99 we saw the stomach churning pictures of Blair posing like some dick head macho-man in the cockpit of a Harrier; in the same month NATO planes bombed an unarmed civilian refugee column of fleeing Kosovo peasants, massacring at least 60 in two separate incidents. The month before NATO planes had bombed a civilian Serb train full of innocent passengers.

When the Real IRA issued its apology for the bomb at Omagh, stating that the innocents were not the intended target, we were treated to mass indignation and outrage by the tabloid press. The same tabloid press which in April '99 gushed platitudes of regret while setting its jaw that such bombing would continue and *inevitably* there would be *many* more such massacres during their bloody campaign in the Balkans. In earlier times in India and in Ireland, British forces quite happily and deliberately killed innocent men, women and children in infamous massacres. They were clearly behind the bombing of Dublin city centre in the late '70s posing as Loyalist terrorists and killing innocent people, and there is more than a hint of suspicion that they actually were behind the ***Birmingham*** bombs; two brothers, the Littlejohns, were the only people in either outrage to be found to be members of any military group, British Special forces, arrested in connection with the bombs, one turning Queen's evidence, pleaded guilty and got off! leaving the six innocent Irishmen to be framed. The IRA have never accepted responsibility for that bombing and there is much to point to the British state itself, which rushed through the Prevention of Terrorism Act without the slightest opposition. So those who weep crocodile tears for the poor victims of republican bombs, give loud ringing cheers when some poor hapless bastard is blown up by British bombs or shot down by British bullets in the name of furthering their political aims by military means.

For us the so-called peace process is a dead end, it is largely a British imperialist ploy to derail the militant republican struggle and at the same time to absorb and disarm politically the people of the republican communities.

For Sinn Fein and the Provos it is a high risk strategy aimed at waiting out the British and playing a numbers game with the catholic population, who in eight years time or so will outnumber the pro-loyalist Protestant community, and they can then "democratically" out-vote the loyalists into a 32 county Irish republic. The loyalists of course, also being democratic, will say "well played sir, you won by the rules". Few people seem to be remembering that this current war started when Sinn Fein won by 75% an all Ireland election in 1918 fought on a home rule ticket. Did the British say well played sir you won by the rules? Nope, they changed the rules and went to war. Republican groups have been fighting ever since in one shape or another.

We do not know the credentials of "Real IRA"; certainly their strategy was entirely fucked up. Given that the vast majority in their community pinned their hopes to Sinn Fein and the peace process, they were going to be operating with a tiny degree of support, which meant any military strategy had to be meticulously planned so as to bring no backlash from their own community. A high profile assassination, or a strike at a military target, might have kept the option for armed struggle on the agenda; a bomb in the middle of the busy shopping centre, trusting the British security forces themselves to pass on the warning and clear the street, on the other hand, was handing them a gift they might have prayed for. It gave them the opportunity to stamp on any talk of military resistance or opposition to the peace process for some considerable time, if not forever. To that extent at least, the British state itself is complicit in the bombing, though they may well have penetrated Real IRA with provocateurs planning the bombing, and the slaughter and setting up the organisation into the bargain. The outrage which followed the indiscriminate slaughter of ordinary folk on the streets of Omagh, genuine enough, though also milked for every drop of tragedy the media and bourgeois politicians could play it up for, removed any area of support for the continuation of armed struggle at this stage. This has now been recognised by the INLA and its political wing the IRSP, who have declared an unconditional end to their armed campaign.

It must also be said the Serb state's war against the people of Kosovo is of the same nature and intent as US / British inspired NATO war against the Serb people, both are acts of imperialist aggression and power-mongering by well heeled self interested politicians. The right of self- determination for the people of Kosovo is a fundamental demand we support, while condemning the manipulating self serving involvement by the big capitalist powers pursuing their own hypocritical agenda. It brings our slogan *NO WAR BUT THE CLASS WAR* back into sharp relevancy.

We regret the loss of innocent working class life, we continue to believe the oppressed and poor have the right to wage struggle in whatever way appropriate and efficient against the state and its armed bodies of men.

On the other side the major downside has been the route of 'progressive' strands among the young loyalist military who were quietly opening doors to thoughts and concepts long ago bolted shut by lies and bigotry, backed up by the armed whereforall to defend new ideas of working class, anti Imperialist, socialistic Protestant traditions. From the outside at least this thin but encouraging strand of dissidence seems to have been prematurely severed by old guard forces who had likewise stemmed all previous attempts among 'loyalist' ranks to examine their history and present and future. It seems unlikely but true that when progressive Communistic tendencies again start to re-emerge among the young of the loyalist communities, it will be among the former members of the para-military groups and the young working class people they formerly recruited from.

 In some Latin American countries where no credible political party exists and the unions have been crushed or operate undercover we have seen lay revolutionary catholic priests abandon pie in the sky to demand food today, we have seen churches used to open inter community debate and discussion on questions of sexism, racialism and hopes for a new world today, not heaven tomorrow.

 Starting October '95 France ground to a standstill every couple of two or three weeks as millions upon millions of workers joined the joint Unions general strike against welfare cutbacks, attacks on the health service and pensions and general austerity measures. Only a tiny fraction of the strikers were Union members, the rest used the Unions as a catalyst around which to focus action as they had in '68. Joined by millions of students and pensioners, the country is systematically brought to a standstill in a rolling political general strike. A month later Unions in Swaziland, southern Africa, continue their general strike against the Monarchy's state of emergency and ban on political parties, demonstrations and free speech. All of the population, including little corner shops, utilise the Unions for their progressive political struggle while supermarkets, banks and businesses reluctant to join the action have their water and electricity supply sabotaged. Participants' views for an alternative vary from workers taking control of society directly to those wishing to install a bourgeois democracy without a constitutional monarch.

Beginning in Jan '96 hundreds of thousands of Russian coal miners joined by 400,000 teachers launch an unlimited general strike against the government's failure to pay any state employee wages and against the general impact of capitalist 'reforms' in general. Suddenly the strike recognises no frontiers and crosses over into Ukraine and then on to Romania. The miners becoming a catalyst for overt political struggle, albeit wage centred, for the class at large. By Jan '97 the French lorry drivers blockade of every roadway, motorway and cycle path had won serious improvements to the terms and conditions of the drivers. While British TV screens fumed at the impotence of the French army and police, drivers in other European countries started to pick up the action. The blockade had begun in November of '96; by the end of dispute more than 250 road blocks were in operation, with army and police vehicles frozen to the tarmac along with everything else. The action won retirement at 55 on full pension, a lump sum, and payment when the driver isn't needed to drive. At least that was what the major bosses agreed, but true to their word some of the biggest ones didn't pay up and in 1997 the road blocks went up again with some spectacular British frothing at the mouth Righteous Brothers 'man in the street' commentary. Monty Pythonite, "bloody reds, it's not safe to drive the roads of Europe these days, road blocks, burning lorries, people protesting, not like that in Britain" they said, until the beef crisis took impoverished Welsh hill farmers into copycat style action over their dispute about livelihoods, and then again as British lorry-drivers blockaded London and then most major cities in protest at Blair's fuel tax.

To be fair to British working class lorry drivers, the few who exist, it was not them who stormed before TV channels over their French 'colleagues' but the majority petit-bourgeois owner-drivers who have sold their souls in a Thatcherite dream of individualism and greed, well used to running over Dockers, Seafarers, Coal Miners, Printers, roads protesters, anti nuclear campaigners, tree lovers and protectors of all things fluffy and furry or anyone else who the state says "break a strike, run the picket and earn a buck" to, they are shocked rigid that French police will not (yet) shoot down protesters and strikers as Maggie would undoubtedly have done were such a crisis at home (It must be said, though this isn't the point here; the '97 action was prematurely and entirely undemocratically undersold by the Biggest French Union after leaning by Mr Blair and Brown on their French "comrades", Who have come to take up Thatcher's banner and demolish "The Unions", actually the working classes' abilities to defend themselves). Spanish Public Sector Unions had been holding monster demonstrations in the capital with crowds of 250,000 plus one day strike actions continued from '96 into '97 joined by other state employees against the State imposed wage freeze.

The revolutionary potential in such developments fair throws itself at you, but there are those so blind as will not see.

For myopic purists like the crowd behind the now late and unlamented *SUBVERSION*, the world of mass struggle was just too impure, too dirty, to be anything other than dismissed. Hatred for "nationalism" becomes total opposition to "nationalist organisations", thereafter all anti-imperialist anti colonial struggle engaged in by a mass of humanity, downtrodden certainly as workers and peasants and just basically starving humanity, but also as peoples of exploited nationalities, can be ignored as irrelevant, even counter revolutionary! After all, "black struggles" are to do with ethnicity, with race, with several black nationalities being oppressed by Imperialism *within* the imperialist states, the USA, & Britain. Of course black people for example are oppressed by and large as a class, but there is an undeniable racial, national element too which white so called revolutionaries ignore at their political integrity peril.

For Subversion, the thought that all are oppressed equally, white, black, brown or Chinese, third world and advanced capitalist state, dying of malnutrition before your first birthday or watching a colour TV in a sumptuous living room, becomes a reality and such things as anti-imperialism, racial exploitation, third world struggles become irritating diversions. Needless to say, Subversion, so called, always ends up arguing against and frequently with the actual people and forces doing the fighting. The IRA fighting the British state's bloody occupation of Ireland can be presented as "the same as" the British state's own army. This of course is true of everyone and anyone who, guns in hand, seeks to get the British state's bloodthirsty talons off its back. Union struggle? Forget it. Unions are "the same as" the bosses, unions (no difference here between workers and leaders) are the enemy of working people and have to be fought and destroyed. For people such as Subversion the vast majority of working class and exploited people of the globe actually engaging *in* struggle, and very often ferocious struggle just to stay alive against the fat cats of Western imperialism and semi colonial plunder, can be dismissed as "not where its at". After all, God loves them, they've not read the paper, have they? Here we sit in splendid isolation not so much like a dog permanently sniffing for its misplaced personal tail around the backsides of its contemporaries, as searching for a body on which to stick the already elaborated head.[14]

It came as little surprise to learn that Subversion had been borne from oot the body of Wildcat, and of necessity bore the distorted birthmarks of such a transition. However the five people who produced Subversion did make efforts to involve themselves in the actual struggles of the class, and it wasn't long before the working class directly were telling our subversive leaders just who would teach who about direction and perspectives, particularly during the heroic Dock workers dispute, subsequently the mass ranks of Subversion descended to 1, and he rapped it up in Autumn 98, suggesting the ACF as a possible home, Eeh well, they all piss in the same pot as we say. The point is, as revolutionary Marxists and Anarchists, if

---

14) The story goes that all the dogs of the world held a world congress of dogs, the first rule of which was all tails had to be hung up at the back of the room to avoid interruption. Some cat conspirator, then started a small fire and shouted Fire! Fire! In the confusion the panicking dogs grabbed any tail on their way out. The result has been that ever since the dogs of the world always start by sniffing each others' bums in an effort to locate their own personal tails. Something of the displaced atomised far flung tribes of Trotskyism seem to function like this, although with Subversion the task is more fundamental having lost its BODY in the confusion of left dissipation.

all we are to do is to span the world and see from one polar cap to the other struggles doomed to failure because of lack or correct organisation, from anti- imperialist struggle to anti racialist struggle to trade union struggle, we will forever and a day be forced to stand on the pavement, as humanity in its array of twisting struggling contingents marches by shouting "You're all doomed! It'll end in tears you know!" Instead we must get into those struggles the people as a whole are taking part in, most certainly point out what our politics and collective experience warn us are dangers and pitfalls, most certainly advance ideas for democratic structures and assemblies and controls, but do it as we fight alongside, not from abstentionist purity.

What About The Labour Party Then?

To throw scorn onto the general class *interventionist* approach sketched above, some have said "well if it's true for Unions, why not then the Labour Party?" We shall leave aside the qualitative differences between a political party, even a mass political party of workers with a particular joint political association, and that of a union which is composed entirely of workers as a whole, and deal with the analogy such as it is. Firstly IF a Labour Party had the active participation of masses of workers centralising around and within the party *in an endeavour to carry through a genuine socialist transition of society and the destruction of capitalism.* Whether we as revolutionaries believed its programme genuine, or if it was, whether it could carry through the task is perhaps matterless, if the mass of workers were convinced it was. We, like it or not, should have to direct our views toward such fellow workers, certainly exposing the dangers of political parties, even where an honest working class one could be found. Certainly we point out the inability of a Capitalist institution like Parliament to carry through its own death warrant, let alone how the state apparatus as a whole would respond. Recognising the impending collision of social classes, albeit in a confused and perhaps naive trajectory, we should have to prepare for a military response, be ready to organise in our communities and workplaces for a true revolutionary situation which would break out not within the hallowed halls of Westminster (although it is possible the state would dispense with parliament itself and give it the recent treatment of the Russian parliament) but on the streets and workplaces. We should be helping in the direct construction of democratic mass assemblies of workers and communities. We should be helping in the co-ordination of the direct takeover of the means of production, distribution and exchange without any legislative acts of parliament.

The wealth and the means of wealth are ours; whose permission do we seek for repossessing it? IF such a party existed which had the degree of naive honesty for the masses of the people to be centred around it, and a programme no matter how limited by our own standards but nonetheless was revolutionary even in a defacto sense, neither us nor the ruling class would be in a position to ignore it, or simply ridicule it as not fitting our preordained "model". A whole moment of history would be unfolding around us, how would we be part of it, what would be our contribution? It would be to *impel* the process forward to its revolutionary climax. The mass of the people would be imposing their own agenda, and as part of that class, as a revolutionary current of that class, *we would be forced to address it.*

WE SHOULD NEED TO PHYSICALLY, INCLUDING MILITARILY, PREPARE FOR THE DEVELOPMENT OF THE REAL REVOLUTIONARY SITUATION ENGENDERED BY THE CONTRADICTORY PROCESS DESCRIBED ABOVE.[15]

To some extent, repeat to _SOME_ extent many of us in the '70s could see things moving in that sort of direction, the militant Trade Union movement, and to an extent the revolutionary left and whole swathes of the class itself, outside the Labour Party, were sending shock waves crashing through its left wing which in turn was impacting on the party as a whole. Theo Sander goes back 23 years to mock my contemporary comments of the period and quotes me: "Left inside the Labour Party started to gain ground." The unmistakable sign of this at that year's Labour Party Conference was "the really big vote for nationalisation of one hundred

---

15) Some of us by the mid '70s were already engaged in embryonic armed and self defence training. It is a story as yet untold, but current class fighters will not be surprised that while respectable numbers of young (and not so young) working class men women and children from every part of the island took up serious military training, we were never able to convince ANY of the numerous self declared "revolutionary organisations" to show any interest in preparation, no matter how minimal, for armed insurrectionary struggle, not even inter faction Karate contests or city orientation courses! This is one aspect of the revolution which "The Vanguards" assumed would "just happen". The quickest way to get a seat in a pub crowded with such 'revolutionaries' was to introduce strongly the question of armed struggle. This was demonstrated by our comrade David O Connell, in a Bridge Hotel, Newcastle meeting, on Ireland. The room abounded with IMG, IS, Militant, CPGB, and the followers of Mao. "I'm sick of all the talking aboot Ireland" shouted Dave pulling out a big revolver "Lets dey something!" the massed ranks of the revolution, crying "my God, he's got a gun!" stampeded in all directions.

monopolies without compensation and under workers' control"[16] So does a resolution for nationalisation without compensation under workers' control backed by millions of votes reflect anything of the overall development of political consciousness? Does it not even feature in an analysis of contemporary events? It means nothing at all?? Or does it, as the full text suggests, reflect the overall class combativity prevalent on the streets, in the workplace and within the party, around which masses of workers were still addressing themselves. I (among others) *also* wrote in 75 "A Labour Government can play the bosses' game as well as the Tories and the workers have shown no special treatment for these governments, being quite prepared to fight whoever it is in parliament if they are serving the interests of capital. They seek to impose their will on the party *in general* not as members inside, but as an independent force acting as a class by means of strikes, factory take-overs, demonstrations etc. It is true to say that many Labour Party Wards are totally apolitical, consisting of a great many paternalists and people who believe in social work etc. The discussion of national politics, to say nothing of the world, is considered out of order and irrelevant against the background of the usual discussions, on the numbers of lamp posts, zebra crossings and allocation of a new car park or two."[17]

Ian MacGreggor years later was to complain, "We had reports of these cadres mainly of young miners based in Doncaster Area being created and trained but we did not realise how effective they would be until the battle for Nottingham was on in earnest" (The Enemy Within, Ian MacGreggor).

It is against the conflicting contradictory struggle that the mass votes for such a resolution were cited as an example of the overall process.[18] Lest someone fears contamination from a less than right - on street cred, nobody is saying here you had to join the Labour Party! Only that this was a general left moving process mirrored to an extent in the Labour Party *AT THAT TIME*. It is also true much of the revolutionary youth of that generation had rejected the Labour Party and adopted more revolutionary bodies, taking direct action and talking the language of anti- and extra-parliamentarianism.

To an extent the Labour Party leaned left because of the prevailing winds - not to have done so would have broken many of its branches from its structure, as indeed many were to be mercilessly lopped off as the wind first died down then turned. At that time, the left moving Labour Party, in a sea of growing revolutionary organisations and consciousness, rocked by the restless militancy within the Unions and the rank and file, DID pose a potential crisis for the ruling class, DESPITE its leadership and history. But whereas a similar process at play in Chile led to a CIA-inspired right wing military coup and the assassination of the elected social democratic president Allende, in Britain the Labour Party leadership had no intention of sowing the wind or reaping any whirlwinds. Concerned though they were that Wilson might not back off, concerned that the young bloods in the factories, the mines and colleges might

---

16) Theo Sander. Rise and Decline of the Shop Stewards Movement as a Mediating Force, in Goodbye To The Unions, Exchanges Et Mouvement.

17) Manifesto Of The Socialist Union Internationalist, Pt One 2nd Edition Aug. '75.

18) At the time of helping write that pamphlet I would doubtless have regarded myself as a Trotskyist though none of us were ever of the "orthodox" varieties.

start directly seizing back the means of production BEFORE any parliamentary "nationalisation", the ruling class prepared its own military coup. Fronted up by elements of MI5 and Brigadier Kitson's "anti insurgency squads" funded by the McWhirter twins and their industrial network, they approached Lord Mountbatton to be the public face of military Government acting constitutionally in the name of Her Majesty. Covert actions by state forces and bodies of armed men were in action at all levels of The State both official, secret and utterly criminal in the '84-85 miners' strike, including terrorist and agent provocateur activities which involved violence, arson and murder, quite apart from the major international and counter information strategy aimed at defeating the strike and the Miners' Union along with its principled leaders.[19]

To this day that constitutional right remains, to dismiss *any* government, to draft in *any* government, draft any law, repeal any law. The armed forces, the police force, the uniformed volunteer organisations ALL swear allegiance to the monarchy, not to parliament. This is not some historic oversight, but a precaution they have retained along with the Monarchy itself, for just such an unlikely eventuality as a 'Labour' government actually committed to wide scale expropriation of capitalism. The strange demise of Diana Princess Of Wales would not have been the first MURDER of disruptive awkward members of the ruling classes deck of kings and queens, British history is full of them, a majority of British people actually believe the Queen and the Establishment had her 'beheaded' and much of the public outpouring which the Windsors tried to capture once the sentiment couldn't be contained was a protest *against* the whole institution of monarchy rather than a grief at the loss of one of *our* sacred royals. Like all struggles the PR job ably assisted by the incoming Mr Blair defeated in the end that progressive sentiment, and dragged 'the Nation' behind the throne again, though at a price, easy to pay, a reformation of the British Monarchy engendering surrender of some power and independence to the Prime Minister, withering away of the House of Lords, together with a big PR job to 'modernise' the position of The Royals, though not of course, God forbid, Abolish it. Blair sees the state's need to retain this option and seeks to soften it a little, lest the public in its spontaneous expression of long held hatreds will not countenance it any longer.

Of course there is a sizeable chunk of the ruling class's periphery to which the Monarchy strikes a resonance and could pose a strong counter-revolutionary balance of reaction. The Countryside Alliance, which at the beginning of '98 mobilised an army of 200,000 of Britain's most reactionary forces, demonstrates how deeply forelock touching and toadying is this sector of society which could always be relied upon at a chosen moment to come to the aid of the State. A comprehensive poll showed 79% of the march were Tory Voters, to all intents and purposes this <u>was</u> the Conservative Party on the march, it comprised not only the "whack 'em and bash 'em" brigade, the landed gentry and their servants, serried ranks of colonel Blimps

---

19) They need not however have worried, Wilson's ear was already blistered by more conventional forces, a hostile press campaign, native and multi-national "strikes of capital", withdrawal of finance, pulling out and the IMF openly threatened to "cripple" the economy if he dared proceed with his programme such as it was. He didn't, and instead the Wilson government opted to continue its "special relationship" with the USA's genocidal war in Vietnam, along with a programme of anti-union legislation, social welfare cuts, attacks on universal education etc. etc.

and retired army types, of course the blood sport enthusiasts, the hunters, the bird killers, the chasers of little furry things and basically everyone who just likes killing things, with dogs, guns, nooses, crossbows, knives or their bare hands. These were happily joined by their militant wing, the British Movement, the Nazis, the Ulster Loyalists, and The UDM (the blackleg organisation set up by Thatcher to split the miners' Union) & whose General Secretary spoke to the rally. Stick this lot in with a call to rally around some right wing Monarchist movement and you begin to see the kind of hideously reactionary role such a centre could play. In the case of Chile (The so called 'British parliamentary system' of South America) Allende nationalised 90% of all foreign industry including strategic copper, tin and zinc and ITT without compensation. The US Fleet was off the coast; within weeks the president lay shot to pieces and democracy was dispensed with.

But if such was the backdrop to those radical resolutions in the '70s what would current trends and directions of the Labour Party reflect? Anything at all, or are political developments and trends just unassociated accidents which 'happen'. On the other hand would they show the utter capitulation of the Parliamentary Labour Party and its leadership (and indeed much of its membership) to the Tory Press agenda, to the politics of the so called 'radical right', the utter abandonment of any vestige of 'socialistic' measures or even liberal social policies? No more anti the bomb, anti NATO, instead support Trident, the EFA, & nuclear weapons proliferation. Be a supporter of New Labour, bomb an Arab or a Serb! Forget the old CND badge, wear the good old Union-Jack and Stars and Stripes. No more incorporation of Unions, even as a sop, instead maintain and build on anti Union laws. Ditch early visions of universal health care, of a pension on which old folk could live in dignity, to hell with equal educational opportunities, long live the public school and educational privilege.

Turn up the Law and Order heat, build more prisons, turn the screws on claimants, witch hunt 'inefficient teachers', propose a curfew on kids in working class districts, compulsory homework detention, retain the privatised industries and allow the corporate thieves to keep their millions. Yes, such is a reflection of the hefty defeats suffered by the organised workers' movement and with them millions more unorganised workers. Its reflects the dog eat dog attitude of the Thatcher years where greed was paraded in print, on screens, in schools and colleges as being a virtue.

If the '70s resolutions reflected the general revolutionary mood outside, so today's dominant trends in the Labour Party reflect the triumph of much of Thatcher's agenda within the Labour Party leadership. It also reflects the change in middle class and petty bourgeois attitudes (increasingly the constituency of new Labour Party members) away from warm liberal feelings for 'fairness and equality' toward hard nosed 'stand on your own two feet' selfishness. Similarly the composition of the Labour Parliamentary Party, once heavily laced with traditional blue collar proletarian rooted MPs, is now the domain of the professional career politician. The purge on leftist northern MPs by the LP leadership finds its expression in candidates imposed on constituencies who have voted for popular characters of their own choice, but are found too uncouth, left or proletarian for the New Labour image. The public school boy, which of course Blair is himself, is more the current model required.

In brief, whatever the trends that may or may not have existed on the ground in the Labour Party of the '70s,perhaps our perceptions were a little over exhilarated by the "something in the air" that trend has been decisively defeated, the nature of the Labour Party now warrants no illusions by anyone. I know of nobody, not least the long suffering die hard Labour Party progressives themselves, who believe the Party has the slightest design in moving one iota away from current Tory policies, or one step toward 'socialism' nomatter how wide you threw the definition. So to answer. Each situation needs to be weighed on its merits, it is a question of analysis of all contending forces, and whereas I can demonstrate Unions are still combat organisation of the working class, and indeed in many cases are essential organs of class self defence, there is no such contribution to be made by The Labour Party, it is doubtful if there ever was, at least so far as the Leaderships were concerned despite the fact that many millions of working class people believed there was and have seen, (and still see in many northern and Celtic regions) voting Labour as a working class gesture of class loyalty and centralism.

There are few who haven't had this knocked out of them now especially after the most decisive right wing victories at the '95 conference, although here and there in the back rooms of northern pubs, a few wards still meet and actually discuss socialism and class struggle, even singing The Red Flag at the end of the meeting. Even these determined souls will soon be driven out as just too old fashioned and embarrassing for the new yuppie image. Blair is the natural successor to Wilson, Callighan and Kinnock in their rightward trajectory. This doesn't mean the Labour Party as a *bourgeois* party supported by millions of workers will disappear, with 600,000 NEW members by 1995 a lot of people of various classes who became so sick of the Tories & felt a change would be as good as a rest are destined to see little of either, other than an embarrassed John Major wondering who nicked his political clothes. Since this pamphlet was initiated we have had the landslide election of a 'New Labour' government, despite the transparency of its anti-working class programme and obvious thorough endorsement by the city and big business, millions upon millions sick of Mk 1 Tories, voted in the hope that a change no matter how slender would be a rest from austerity and repression it is wishful thinking born of 19 years of defeat and poverty.

What is unpardonable is the disgraceful peddling of the 'Vote Labour, but ...' line presented by our 'leaders' in the SWP, WP, CPB, etc. Such vanguards show themselves to be miles behind advanced sectors of the anti-Tory working class, who have abstained from voting as a POLITICAL action against the whole parliamentary diversion and know this Mk 2 Tory government will have to be fought with equal determination on the streets, communities and workplaces as the official Tories. The attacks upon the poor, the working class in general, on sexual freedoms, on the liberties of the young, on the sick, old and disabled are monstrous continuations of the Thatcher years, which another Tory Tory government couldn't have dreamed of fulfilling. Blair is a loyal continua of Thatcher, attacking the crippled miners' benefits, the single parents, the unemployed, the disabled, poor working class communities of impoverished and alienated children and young people and unleashing a war against drugs, beggars, homeless, sexual 'promiscuity' children playing on streets, hippies, protesters - the list never ends. NOW do we know "VOTE LABOUR, BUT ..." as a slogan means "This way to kick yourself and your friends up the arse, and do the dirty on the poorest people in society". It seems our 'comrades' in the left parties, if by some fluke an election were to be held tomorrow, would still serve us the same utterly poisoned chalice. We would, likewise, say the same as we did: ORGANISE THE POOR, THE PEOPLE OF NO PROPERTY, THE PEOPLE OF DISABILITY, AND FIGHT THE TORIES - LABOUR, LIBERAL OR CONSERVATIVE! It is entirely clear that it was never us that was 'ultra-left' or paranoid, but now that the bastards are kicking your door down, it must be obvious that you welcomed them in! - whereas, quite correctly, you would never have spit on a burning Tory. We must enforce the realisation that Labour shite does stink, and Labour/Liberal Tories are the same as the old kind. If we want to keep the few things our parents and grandfolk won for us, we must fight again, together as a class, by all means necessary, OURSELVES, and trust no-one but ourselves.

A Socialist Labour Party?

Illustrative of the way in which working class organisation can rapidly change form and move into unexpected areas creating a new agenda has been the way in which the idea of forming a Socialist Labour Party caused an excited ripple to spread through leftist sections of the class. Totally and finally disgusted with 'Tory' Blair's open acceptance and advocacy of Thatcherite policies, the destruction of the last shreds of any procedures and their replacement by a virtual Leader dictatorship, the scrapping of all socialistic policies finally cemented by the ritual public slaughter of Clause Four pt four many have cried enough! Centred around the charismatic and influential leadership of Arthur Scargill the debate had been opened up around plans for the new party, a principled working class organisation directly challenging 'New Labour'. As soon as the call hit the streets it lit a spark throughout the working class communities. In northern cities, in pubs, shops, and clubs debate around the local football fixtures, love affairs and lottery results was peppered with discussion on "Scargill's new party".

Not for many a year had anyone seen so many ordinary usually non political people debate class organisation, and whether Labour new or Socialist or either offered any way forward for the working class. Phone-in programmes in Newcastle, Hull, Sheffield, and Leeds were flooded with callers trying to make their respective points, it being noted that they were two to one in favour of a new working class organisation and against New labour. The '96 Hemsworth by-election seemed to present an early challenge and Brenda Nixon of Women Against Pit Closures decided to take on the 'official' labour candidate. Having given itself less than 10 days to mount a campaign nobody seriously expected Brenda (least of all her) to storm into parliament on the crest of a left-labour wave. To our Anarcho-Marxist wing of class politics numbers of votes are of little qualitative importance in themselves, but it is a simple fact she might easily have gained the few hundred extra votes required to come second, with all the physiological and propagandist value that would have delivered. That this wasn't achieved was due entirely to Leader-Centrism and Arthur's absolute obsession with supervising and checking everything himself for fear of far left contamination. One of the reasons why people in our camp stand well clear of political parties is precisely the tendency to bureaucracy, ego-centricity and internal wrangles over who should be boss.

What is incidentally amassing (although perhaps shouldn't be) is the way in which self declared 'revolutionary' groups like SWP have *condemned* the break away from Blair's New Labour, virtually defending it as 'the workers party' against socialists arguing for a more radical platform. That Benn and Skinner with a lifetime role as 'loyal leftist opposition of the Palace of Westminster' should take such a stance is understandable, that self declared revolutionaries should do it is unprincipled and opportunist to a fault.

The first thing to say about the situation in general was that it was an extremely healthy sign, putting back on the agenda of ordinary folk the question of working class organisation and opening up arguments over which type of programme and perspective. It had to an extent opened a window in a room of dusty conservatism and decay. Industrial Unionists such as myself were able to enter the debate and pose our perspectives of direct working class struggle in a climate of renewed political interest. As a guest spokesperson from the pit communities and representative of the NUM Branch which moved a resolution to the 1996 NUM Annual Conference that the Union disaffiliate from the Labour Party, I have been an invited speaker on a number of the phone-in.'s, posing more radical solutions to class struggle than those presented by a left Labour Party.

The original Socialist Labour Party was Industrial Unionist, Revolutionary Marxist and anti-parliamentarian. The new SLP is none of these, having survived the bureaucratic conditions of its birth it has no problem standing to the left of New Labour on everything, it *is* thoroughly more working class in composition than probably any of the left groups and certainly strikes a more popular cord with the class than the SWP / WRP or any other of the self declared saviours of the class. SLP candidates received a total of 52,110 votes nationally with an average of 1.85% in the '97 General Election, given that individual candidates with far left credentials such as Iran Khan took 6.76 % of the vote, and many others had respectable returns despite the mass abstention by many advanced sectors of the working class. In the 1998 by-election for Barnsley's Worsbrough Ward, Ann Scargill, quite the most honest and dedicated person in the whole organisation took the Party to second place, with 17.1 % of the vote (however 75% of voters made a conscious choice to register NO vote) it is clear some form of revolutionary message *still* strikes a cord despite years of de-politicising, de-classing, debilitating state propaganda even within this mind chillingly boring arena, demonstrates a clear potential for genuine revolutionary class struggle organisations.

Having said that, the organisation is already malformed by an unnatural breach birth and bureaucratic manoeuvrings and behind the scenes posturing which already has served to dampen the original joyous tones of the christening. Comrade Scargill was determined that the constitution be drafted in his own image and likeness, that this should be approved BEFORE the founding conference, that a special IN CROWD form the central caucus and have the whole thing stage managed before any of the raggy arse revolutionaries waiting to join could cry "Comrade Chair, we object!" Crucial in the infant's deformity is the obsession by Arthur and the leadership to keep tendencies and factions OUT of the new organisation. Something which Old Labour did with clause four pt five in 1921 with the bans and prescriptions rule. It is a feature which will ensure leftist groups such as Militant Labour and the remnants around the CPGB will be unable to throw their not insignificant weight and organisation capacities into the new organisation, something which in objective terms it needed, to continue its momentum.

Since its foundation the bureaucratic manoeuvring and scandalous exclusion and expulsion (the old Stalinist trick is to say the dissident member ISN'T a member and never was one) of leftists has continued with a force old Reg Prentice would have cheered as the ranks of 'voided' individuals and now even whole branches gets longer. The hapless delegates to the organisations' first conference, foolishly thinking they could actually vote for direction and change, were rudely awakened by the discovery that one delegate had 3,000 votes solidly behind Arthur on every issue. The Lancashire Miners Association,whose leadership were members of the SLP, had apparently affiliated the whole organisation and comfortably ensured that Arthur and Co. would have their own way on everything from Constitution, to policies on race and sex. A very clear lesson of the dangers of political parties even at the early stage of their lives. Think what such a creature would be like in office let alone power!

Since the original drafting of the above paragraphs, already by Feb. '98 the SLP is entirely bureaucratic and deformed, at least as a participatory party of the working class is concerned. As Arthur's Fan Club, or a Retirement Home for ex-Stalinists, exTrotskyists, Union officials and some activists, it continues. Insofar as working class people pissed off with obscenity of New Labour are concerned the superficial message is still nice, nostalgic and even inspiring; it will earn a clap, a standing ovation, and maybe votes in any future election. As a pivot for organising 'the Left' it might stand a conference or two, but essentially as a real vehicle for change, that bolt was misfired, that moment has gone, for this team anyway. Many will still clutter to its glow, but that glow tends sadly to be Arthur's, and not the real daylight; moths would tell you, if they could, what a mistake that is! Trust NO-ONE BUT The working class together, ourselves, and at liberty, to be what we want, say what we want and decide what we want TOGETHER. Our organisations, when we build them, are for us, together, not for leaders, not for executive committees, not for special conferences of special people. Rules, when we have rules - and sometimes we need them - WE ALL DECIDE ON, and the first rule is OTHER OPINIONS MUST BE HEARD, before we decide what we think together.

Our history of momentous struggle and inspired visions is littered and polluted with dictatorships and leaderships, ruling groups and constitutions which have robbed us at every vital juncture of our own collective control of events. Not all leaders and visionaries are doomed to be traitors, ONLY IF we the mass of the people hold absolute control and power to ensure that they do not get the chance, or occasion, to test that view.

Scottish Socialist Alliance
(now the Scottish Socialist Party, we believe)

The Scottish version of the SLP which went its own way because of the shenanigans south of the border, is a qualitatively healthier creature than its sasanach sister, in terms of tendency and faction rights, open debate and a punchier programme. In election terms it faired similar to its English brother achieving 9,740 votes and 1.83% of the vote on average. In extra parliamentary terms it seems to be having the effect of uniting much of the left nationalist with Old Scottish left and Red Clyde & post war Stalinist traditions as well as broad areas of Trade Union activists. Such is a heavy broth for us to swim in, but we should undoubtedly use the opportunities of renewed debate and enlivened interest in class politics (albeit heavily parliamentarian and social-democratic at this stage) to advance our own ideas for workers direct control and ownership and the revolutionary capture of power outwith the confined and constraints of parties and parliament.

Class Relationships

Having drawn attention to the multi-dimentional nature of revolutionary struggle, it is necessary to recognise the centrality of the workplace and economic mode of production to the whole conflict. It is this feature which is central to the whole class relationship. It is the transaction of the workers selling their labour power to the employer, in order to live, and the employer buying that labour power in order to make a profit, which is the base on which the capitalist economic system and the 'wage slavery' which underpins it nests. This is not of course to suggest that class exploitation is one dimensional, we are exploited on every level of life and existence, at home, in school, in social and sexual relationships, it impacts in every way, in perceptions of art, animals and each other, but the whole of those value relationships and modes of exploitation are underpinned and indeed developed from the economic mode of production dominant in society.

Get the question of this fundamental element in the class relationship wrong and you've blinded yourself to any other question you care to look at. For this reason it is essential that we keep our feet on the ground and not be led off into self imposed irrelevance by adopting ultra-leftist sounding 'anti-union' positions, which at best confuse working people or else totally alienate them from Anarchist and revolutionary Marxist politics. Of late we see petit bourgeois elements "discovering" that "traditional" (that is the struggle in the workplace) class war is dead. Never ever having fitted in comfortably with the working class, they breath a sigh of relief - now they don't have to be workers to be exploited. The "new class struggle" will embrace them equally with the prol'. The anti-roads protests, animal exports protests, environmental struggles seem to make class origin and orientation irrelevant. Of course it doesn't, it is still the class orientation to the underpinning economic mode of production, and the method by which class society will internally combust through the class war itself which is decisive. The mass movement of the working class as a class is still a fundamental requirement of the destruction of capitalism, even if along the way a thousand other issues which affect the general quality of life as "citizens" or "consumers" intervene to mobilise masses of people, in truth they always have, they were just dwarfed by massive industrial struggles of the proletariat.

The three richest individuals in the world have a fortune which is higher than the combined Gross Domestic Product of the 48 poorest nations.

The capital of the 15 richest individuals is higher than the total GNP of Sub-Saharan Africa.

The assets of the 84 richest individuals are higher than China's GNP with 1.2 billion inhabitants.

4% of the combined assets of the 225 largest fortunes world wide, would be sufficient to ensure all inhabitants of the planet access to basic needs and social welfare, health, education and food.

On a world scale 20% of human beings in the richest countries share 85%s of all private consumption in the world, whilst 20% of those living in the poorest countries share 1.3 %

20% of the richest individuals share 45% of all fish and meat consumption, 58% of all energy, 87 % of all vehicles, 84 % of all paper. 74% of all telephone lines, and release 53% of all carbon dioxide into the atmosphere.

20% of the inhabitants of the poorest countries share only 5% of fish and meat consumption, 4% of world energy, 1% of all vehicles, 1.1 % of paper, 1.5% of telephone lines, and release only 3% of carbon dioxide into the atmosphere

90% of the worlds population has NO access to electricity and 1.3 billion people are denied access to drinking water.[20]

Whilst by comparison workers in the 'affluent west' are far better off than their poorer third world comrades, the degree of wealth distribution and perpetuation of the class system within the west of course continues. Somewhere in the region of 12% of the population own 90% of all wealth. Control of share capital, land ownership etc. is similarly concentrated in the hands of this tiny hyper privileged group, the capitalist class. The worker does not *own* anything to make a living, unlike the tramping artisan of the early C19th he does not own his own tools, unlike the cottage industries the workers families do not make whole objects to sell. S/he doesn't own orchards from which to take carts of apples or pears to sell at market. They have only their *labour power* to sell, and this must be rationed out and sold like apples or the whole product at the highest possible price. On the other side the capitalist or more. likely his management representative seek as much labour as possible and at the smallest possible price in order to extract the greatest labour power from it. Around this conflict the class war takes place. Taken as individuals the boss can force the worker to fling his cap on the table and beg for work, almost at any price if s/he has been out of work long enough (this is, of course, the purpose of *THE POLICY* of unemployment). It is for this reason that combinations of workers, later to be called Unions, have evolved, by forming a collective, a microcosm of the class as such, by advancing the collective class interest and setting a minimum of wages and conditions under which no-one should work. In the pamphlet <u>Anarchism And The Trade Unions,</u> Workers Solidarity Movement, our Irish comrades demonstrate qualitatively more maturity than their southern English counterparts:-

20) International Energy & Miners Organisation Newsletter Aug-Sept 1998, quoting United Nations Conference on Trade and Development report 1998.

"The workers who create the wealth under capitalism are different to all previous oppressed classes. They have to fight together if they are to win and they can only achieve their freedom together. The small peasants of Ireland in the last century did fight together at times, particularly in The Land League agitation. But the goal of the small peasant was to become a bigger peasant and then an independent small farmer. Modern workers can not share such a goal. They can not break up large industries, power, supermarkets, hospitals, railways, schools and so on, and share them out piece by piece among themselves. They can only control production and essential services collectively.

"This means that the working class can be a force capable not merely of rebelling against the existing system but of taking over and recreating society in their own interests. As the majority class the modern working class can not become a ruling class in the way that the merchants replaced the feudal lords. There wouldn't be enough people for them to exploit and live off, even if such an idea became popular. The victory of the working class will see it having to dissolve itself and usher in a truly classless society.

"Trade Unions were first organisations thrown up by the working class in struggle against the bosses. Trade Union are essentially, defence organisation of workers under capitalism. Their very existence is a challenge to the right of the boss to set wages and conditions of work. Nomatter how conservative, bureaucratic or downright backward a union may be, to join it implies a recognition that there is a class division in society and that workers have to get together to fight for their own separate interests. This is a sign of some level of class consciousness."[21]

Our critics, ostensibly on the left, would say that inherently this relationship recognises as normal the wage slavery of capitalism and all we are doing is making the best of a bad deal. In truth there is nothing, in the temporary 'deal' we have to make on the best terms for now which says, or even implies, we aren't coming back for the lot! Nothing! Individual leaders, professional bureaucrat parasites and even many workers may well accept capitalism as being the normal state of affairs and to which there is no viable alternative, but a huge number of working people, and even on occasion Trade Union leaders, likewise do not.

There is nothing to stop workers, through their unions, or independent rank and file bodies aspiring to *The Abolition of the wages system itself.* But what about RIGHT NOW? In trying to persuade comrade Brendel as to why, should he have ever chanced upon the shop floor of a factory forced to earn his living by selling his labour, he too would join the Union, because the price of that labour would depend upon strength of the union. So too his conditions of safety, what if he were to loose his fingers in a machine, who would fight for compensation and improved standards? To which Cajo responds as if going to work were a simple matter of choice. "Do you really want me (or anybody else) to believe that anyone could possible be interested in compensation? Parents whose child has been run over by a car could be interested in "compensation"? The family of a miner who has been killed in a mine accident could be interested in "compensation"? If I lost a finger or a hand because of unsafe machinery I

21) Anarchism And The Trade Unions, Op Cit.

could be interested in "Compensation"? You must be joking - or you must be one of these union officials completely out of touch with reality to sincerely believe in such nonsense - I want all my ten fingers and both hands, I want to be perfectly healthy as well, and if I am in danger of being hurt or mutilated by any unsafe machinery, then I want this machinery not to be used until it is completely safe (can you imagine what would happen in the coalmining industry of today if you made this a rule?)"[22] In every other workplace in Britain, Europe and the rest of the world too, yes, and no one shall travel on public or private transport, car, ship, bus, train or plane until we are sure it is not deficient, and the food we eat, we shall not work until it is cleansed of all poisons and impurity, we shall not study, perform, or labour until the air is pollution free and the ozone holes are plugged and the oceans run clean, yes, we should have a world wide general strike, we shall engage in a world revolution and capitalism will dangle its impotence before the eyes of humanity!

But Cajo comrade, I mean what do we do RIGHT NOW! Nobody wants to get up at 4.30 a.m. and go to work in a blizzard, shovelling rock on a water infested coalface in a coal mine either, but it isn't a matter of staying in bed thinking up nicer ways of spending the day. What do we put on the dining table? A copy of Capital, or perhaps we can actually eat Kropotkin's 'Conquest of Bread'? Of course it's obscene to be forced to work in order to live, it shouldn't happen, that's why we are Communists.

Yes there is an answer: **The International General Strike against wage labour, Capitalism and all forms of exploitation and oppression** is one solution, but unless its going to be ready by the time the kids get in from school and want their tea we had better decide to maximise our bargaining power NOW! To maximise the level of the wage NOW! To improve the safety NOW! and yes Win the maximum compensation for death, illness and injury NOW! **_at the same time as_ building for the revolutionary overthrow of capitalism** not as a subsidi-ary, not as 'tomorrow's goal'. but at the same time as dealing with the questions posed by the balance of power now, and the stage of revolutionary class consciousness and organisation now. How are we to achieve improvements in wages, safety and conditions - one by one going into the boss and asking nicely? Of course not, by collective strength, by solidarity, by class action, in Unions.

After all we don't seek work either on principle or for lack of it. But because the bosses have cornered the means of life and we have to work to live The level at which we live is mostly determined by wage negotiation based on the strength of union organisation and the determination of the members collectively.

Trade Unionism at this level is not some academic model, but the ability to put food on the table without flogging your body to death or coming home in a box.

This is why when some comrades ostensibly from 'the left' and 'Anarchist movement' say "We are anti- the Unions", we as workers are dumbfounded.

22) Answer To Dave Douglass, Cajo Brendel, Goodbye To The Unions, Op Cit.

If the IWW hadn't entered negotiations on terms and conditions *and wages* in the here and now it couldn't have been utilised by ordinary workers who while wanting and organising for revolution also needed to live in the meantime. The IWW was an immensely principled organisation; it was equally practical, personally I cannot see what good one is without the other. Those who believe the struggle to defend and advance our terms and conditions now under capitalism is some kind of distraction from 'The Revolution' should reflect on the *old man's* view:-

"the very development of modern industry must progressively turn the scale in favour of the capitalist against the working man, and that consequently the general tendency of capitalistic production is not to raise, but to sink the average standard of wages, or to push the value of labour more or less to its minimum limit. Such being the tendency of things in this system, is this saying that the working class ought to renounce their resistance against encroachments of capital, and abandon attempts at making the best of their occasional chances for their temporary improvement? If they did, they would be degraded to one level mass of broken wretches past salvation ... By cowardly giving way in their everyday conflict with capital they would certainly disqualify themselves for the initiating of any larger movement" (Karl Marx).

We should note that in taking an 'anti-union' stance, 'groups' like Subversion, Wildcat and Communist Workers Organisation also stand against 'Red' or 'revolutionary Unions'.

"This can clearly be seen from union recruitment policy which is to try and sell membership to anybody who will pay the membership dues no matter how reactionary they may be, as long as they work in the right trade/industry. It should be obvious that no working class organisation can operate in this way" Wildcat.[23] The passage is rather like Stephen Norris's statement, the Tory Rail minister; he said he preferred travelling in his car because you didn't get to sit next to obnoxious people. Reactionary workers? Ignore them! Form your own exclusive organisation and keep the toe rags out. Still less does the idea of mass assemblies and mass decision making as a prelude to action suit them "Democracy, with its fetish for the airing of opinions and the moment of decision as a preliminary to acting, offers nothing to workers. It offers everything to those who would divert, institutionalise or block their struggles, whether its the right with their secret ballots or the left with their delegate conferences and mass participatory democracy" (Wildcat).

So, if a worker, (and these people have only the most nebulous of concepts as to what a worker is, let alone how we think and act,) do you:

a) Take whatever the boss is prepared to pay you and say "God bless you"?

b) Don't work for wages at all, go off and join the New Age travellers, or a circus?

c) Live off inherited wealth, don't work, spend your time preaching to workers on how wrong they have this revolution thing?

At least Wildcat is honest in its response to an alternative to unions "The short answer is were not proposing an "alternative" to the unions. If you want to negotiate the rate of

---

23) Curious how something which they don't agree with ipso facto cannot be "working class".

exploitation and reinforce working class corporatism, the unions are an excellent way of doing a difficult job and doing it very well under the circumstances. That's why we hate them."

So £1 an hour or £20 an hour, it's all the same to Wildcat. However that's not the way any worker we ever knew views the situation, and for all Wildcat's revolutionary sounding rejection of everything, the perspective still translates in reality as apathy, or a pathetic "well, what can we do?"

I have nothing but the utmost respect for people who, pissed off with being up against it in a dead end city with no hope of a job, try and live their lives some other way as travellers or whatever. These are not the people who come back to haunt the factory gate and tell workers how useless unions are. Non participation in industrial or workplace struggle is often not a matter of choice, but of being forced out of "the labour market" through endless unemployment queues or redundancy. However building alternative life styles other than working for wages or attempting to work for wages is unlikely to be the main factor in working class struggles in Britain.

For most people the realisation is workers organised together in a collective force have power. The whole purpose of the anti- unions laws is precisely to bring around a state of powerlessness, by breaking the collective organisation, sometimes even by destroying the very industry in which the unions are most powerful and socially challenging. Smashing the union has frequently been a prerequisite to forcing down wages, changing shift lengths and patterns and worsening wage conditions. The converse is also true as strong unions engender higher wages and better working conditions, even sometimes by proxy in non union firms as employers make a conscious choice to pay over the odds in order to keep the union out and workplace dissatisfaction under control. Even in the worse of all times for Unions in Britain today with mass unemployment, viscous anti union laws and a brow beaten Trade Union movement, more than 50% of all people who are working, are in Unions, and tens of thousands of them, at any one time will be on strike in any part of the island. Of course if your "outside and against the Unions" and at the same time offer no alternative to them, such events are unlikely to bother you.

In the Timex dispute we seen two conflicting aspects of *UNIONS*, the manual staff on strike, assisted by workers from all unions and Trades Councils from all over Britain. At the same time white collar MSF members cross the picket lines with the scabs. Union emergency meetings organise to draft in bus loads of supporters to join the picket lines, while MSF at its annual conference votes down a resolution calling for its Timex members to stop crossing the picket lines. Which is the *trade unionism* here? Can the jelly backed creatures who drive to work each day behind an army of police characterise *trade unionism?* Cajo's technique would be to sight the Timex strikers as examples of anti- unionist autonomous action, while the MSF conference would be an example of the treacherous nature of Trade Unionism. But would that be a *realistic* way to view a conflictual process enacted within Unions? How would our anti- Unionists intervene into the massive fight at Wapping to ESTABLISH craft Unionism in the print works against activities of Union busters using the scab EETPU, facing down mounted police and riot shields and snatch squads. Do you roll up and say you support *the workers* but by the way don't agree with Unions, and worse that you are ANTI-UNION? On the docks the Heroic 2 year fight by dockers and their families to defend the fundamental *Trade Union* principle of not crossing picket lines and backing up other workers in struggle, is done to death in part by the counter activities of *Trade Union* leaders in TGWU and others. So the dockers were in 'anti-union' struggle, and Morris is in pro-Union struggle against them? Maybe I'm the one whose missing something here, but I cannot see that as a credible position no-matter how it is viewed. It is not possible to support 'the workers' in abstract, only in practice, and in practice 99.9% of all workplace struggles take place within Unions at one level or another.

CRAFT UNIONISM

Many of the 'left' critics of unions fall back on the old chestnut about craft exclusiveness and sectionalism. We could argue about this word *Trade Unionism* over *Trades Unionism* enough to say Trade, Skill, Labour Aristocracy did exist. My fellow Tynesider Tom Brown mercilessly nailed their weaknesses to the floor in his book <u>Syndicalism</u>. But Tom was a man born to the struggles of industrial Tyneside and never at any point has he or would he call for abstention-ism from trade union struggle if the alternative were non-unionism or isolation from the rest of the class. In any case *Craft Unionism* also had strengths. As the industrial revolution re-quired greater and greater skills, so the labour of such workers became more refined and highly priced. These 'aristocrats' the coopers, the printers, the machine tool makers, the industrial engineers developed extensive areas of job control. Whilst their trades were jeal-ously guarded against dilution, they themselves often developed high levels of <u>class</u> con-sciousness, and many were at the forefront of the political struggles of the class *as a class*. At times their unions have been central to major offensives, the struggles of the engineers in the Nine Hours Movement of the last century. They saw their strong bargaining craft positions as spearheads for the whole movement of labour.

Whilst the exclusive *Trade* unionism of the craft societies restricted the participation of unskilled workers, it is important to realise that these unskilled workers did not by that fact remain unorganised. By the beginning of the C19th forerunners of *Industrial Unionism* were already emerging on the docks, in shipping, and more particularly in mining. Elsewhere the mass of do anything, work anywhere general labourers were forming mass general unions of the unskilled. Although organised in separate societies, all of these unions, almost from their inception, sought mutual co-operation and solidarity. In the 1860s through to the 1890s whole cities would often strike together, across craft and skill divisions.[24]

---

24) My unfinished and as such unpublished research on this question is still in a raw form but it is a clear feature of the last century; 'a general strike' was a fairly common occurrence wherein all workers in a city or even a region would turn out together. So far as I can tell it has been totally ignored by labour historians probably because like much else it doesn't fit into the preconceived idea of what went on. I have very painfully started to re-work this piece and hope maybe to complete it before I kick my clogs. I am

THE TUC

The TUC, which today is an abbreviation for inaction or gutless abject surrender to the bosses, in its concept as a single centre uniting all workers regardless of religion, region, or craft, was a progressive highly advanced concept. Certainly it was qualitatively more refined than the continental Union centres divided along religious, regional and party political lines. I am aware that comrades hold say, the CNT as a model for class organisation, which in abstract it is. However a CNT island a sea of Catholic, Protestant, Socialist, Communist, Christian Democrat unions, *is overall*, weaker. A united working class united in a single centre is quanatively superior and sets the scene for the potential of advancing class consciousness of the whole of the class on a qualitatively higher level. The IWW was for a spectacular period able to do both.

The power given to skilled workers by their crafts, encouraged employers at every stage to find ways of lessening the skill requirements, usually through a change in technology, this was only incidentally 'an inevitable result of science' and more to do with a strategic positioning to rob workers with high bargaining power from their strong class positions.

The struggles of the shear croppers, and the Luddites were an early example, whilst the latest could be seen at Wapping with new computer based multi-de-skilling techniques forced a final encounter with the print unions with their powerful class position and job control and resistance to employer regulation. In the case of the miners, we seen that not even financial considerations effect the change, gas and nuclear power generation far outstripping less costly coal generation, but the class position of the strategically placed miners had to be broken. As technologies have changed the workplace so workers have altered their organisations to retain some collective control, and this has led to the virtual demise of the *craft union* as such. Engineering, Electrical unions for example are more correctly now *General unions* recruiting everybody across whole swathes of industry.

THE TENDENCY TO MERGER which has marked the last twenty years can in some senses be seen as a move back toward industrial type union concepts. UNISON uniting COSHE NUPE and NALGO brought together 1.5 *million* workers in health care and public services. Proposed joining of GMBU with TGWU and possibly UCATT would produce a single union centre covering General, Transport, and Building, construction, tunnelling etc. and be over 2 *million* strong. These are powerful blocks of organised labour and despite bureaucratic structures, and the mish mash of left and centre union traditions, the memberships of these unions see in them features of 'ONE BIG UNION' aspired to by the IWW coupled with rank and file campaigns to win the new formation over to a more radical political position as a whole.

---

narrowing it down to Liverpool as a classic example of an overall trend. General Strikes On The Liverpool Waterfront 1840-90. I am a poor historian insofar as life and struggle in the 1990s and into the new 2000 occupies most of my attentions and, whilst inspiring, as Marx said about history, The Point ... is to change it!

Self Interested Bureaucracies

All Trade Unions have developed bureaucracies, more often than not these have become a dead hand upon workers aspirations to struggle. The bureaucrat sees himself as the guardian of the apparatus, the protector of its funds and institutions, he is a paternalist, who will protect the worker from himself. Usually such functionaries are paid far and away above the wages of the worker he is supposed to represent, with assorted privileges, car allowances, houses, salaries etc. They can and sometimes are forced into action by determined responses by the membership who have usually had to overcome a steeplechase of obstacles and diversions before getting into the fight. Sometimes it happens when the prevailing industrial and political current threatens to sink the union as a whole, with him in it. However in both circumstances the bureaucrat will inevitably still hold back and try and adopt a more concilliationary role, for fear of damaging the apparatus which he has come to hold more dearly than the reason for its existence.

"There does emerge within Trade Unions a strata that develops a professional interest in a partnership with the bosses. This bureaucracy has about as much in common with the found- ers of the trade union movement as Peter Casssells has with James Connolly. These bureau- crats may be elected or unelected, what marks them out is that they have extended powers but are not answerable to the membership except in the most formal way. In reality they are often beyond any control from the rank and file membership."[25]

There are exceptions, but to my knowledge, never *absolute* exceptions. Because of its Indus- trial Unionist structure, with democratic branches and regional bases, and loosely federated national organisation the NUM and its forebears has tended to be more in tune to rank and file momentum to action. On a number of occasions this has taken the organisation up and including total disintegration in battle. Its first three attempts at formation were smashed and the leaders vilified and blacklisted all over the country, many dying in extreme poverty. The fate of the MFGB in '26 and the NUM between '85 and '92-93 has been almost the same with every organisational nut and bolt breaking apart but with most of the leaders committed to a fight to the finish even if it meant the destruction of the organisation.

Greatly weakened by the year long '84 strike when the last offensive came in '92-93 the Yorkshire Area alone, spent in excess of £120,000 on transport for two national demonstra- tions. The Miner and millions upon millions of leaflets called on workers to STRIKE WITH THE MINERS. This was a totally illegal call and for which all of the officials at National and Area level could have faced arrest with the funds confiscated and the union closed down. The fact that members of NALGO and GMB responded and struck, whilst other unions once

---

25) Anarchism and The Trade Unions, Talk given at the Workers Solidarity Movement open discussion in Dublin on May 6th 1992. It should not be implied that this document would agree with my proposition that unions, particularly at base CAN be used for revolutionary actions or as part of a revolutionary *process*. However their grasp on the reality of the work situation and workers involvement through Unions is clearly closely linked to my own perceptions.

more kept their heads below the trench once again demonstrates the different degrees of combativety among the leaders, but also the <u>members</u> directly to whom the call was issued.

My attempts to illustrate the revolutionary periods in the miners history are not attempts to suggest that the miners unions have an unbroken history in that direction. Defeat often led to more moderate voices gaining the ear of the community, and parliament became an early means to find redress rather than the extended strike and gunpowder. The miners have at times fought pitched battles with right wing miners leaders.[26]

I confess that I took it for granted comrades were aware of the more usual, non militant, moderate role of bureaucracies, and endeavoured to show a contrasting function. The recent militant resurgence in the NUM in '72 through to '93 began with the 1969 <u>unofficial</u> national strike.[27] It marked an end to the period of conservative leaderships which had dominated since the time of nationalisation through the '50s and early '60s, but again it should be noted that strike was organised around sections of <u>*the union*</u> in action against the wishes of other sections and areas of <u>*the union.*</u>[28]

Arthur as a matter of fact often lost touch with the membership not from the sell out position but from the opposite pole, calling for industrial action at every turn, regardless of circumstances and the preparedness of the miners. <u>BOTH</u> are the result of a bureaucratic position and occupying social relationships removed from the rank and file. However that is not to say comrade Scargill's sincerity and hatred of capitalism is not real enough, it is. His total commitment to the miners, rather than protection of their instrument (*the union*)[29] was undoubtedly demonstrated in 84-85. Two thirds of the way through that strike most area full time officials knew we should not all live happily ever after, and committed everything, funds, offices, their own positions to an all out, take it to the limit battle, as did the rank and file and their families with homes, jobs in some cases lives and liberty, on the line.

Anyone who has read even briefly a history of the miners unions knows, on a number of occasions the organisation was rammed full force against the class enemy and broken. Reaction to this briefly has been leaders committed to saving the apparatus, building its funds, preserving its offices, Cajo likes to point to such men as examples of Miners Leaders, such have rarely lasted long.

---

26) See my Pit Life In Co. Durham, Rank and File Movements in the Durham Coalfield, Published by The History Workshop, Oxford.

27) Incidentally I discuss this period in my book, jointly authored with Joel Krieger, A Miners Life, published by Routledge and Keegan Paul. I make the point, "the 1969 strike swept aside the old union leaderships and gave birth to a new left leadership". This went on to lay the ground for the struggles of '72 and '74. Theo Sander, without any attempt to match up the dates, concludes that I am here talking about *me*. "This kind of self-congratulatory myth ... peddled by middle aged trade union officials like Dave Douglass". Well, nobody gets any younger comrade, not even you, but the leaderships I was plainly referring to took up position in time for the '72 and '74 offensives, that is the point of the observation. I didn't get elected until a full <u>decade after the old leaderships were "swept aside"</u> in '69. So whoever I am congratulating it is certainly not myself.

28) This illustrated at length in Pit Sense Versus The State, published by Phoenix Press.

29) Yes in this instance we *are* talking of the apparatus, the bricks and mortar as against *the miners* as such.

By the time this pamphlet came to be wrote less than 8,000 miners remain, in 15 pits mostly still in the NUM though some covertly because of the risk of the sack, in 1984 we went into battle with 180,000 miners behind the banners of the NUM. In 1999 our long suffering members voted by 57% to take all out strike action again for Union recognition and increased wages.

We fought to the virtual death, and yet Sue Gupta,[30] author of Analysis talking of our '92-93 campaign can write:-

"IN A SENSE I'M GLAD THE MINERS HAVE BEEN DEFEATED, IF YOU CRAWL ON YOUR BELLY BEGGING FROM THE BOURGEOISIE THEN YOU DESERVE A GOOD KICK IN THE TEETH."

What is incredible is that anyone with the remotest credentials to claim to be a working class revolutionary could give such arrogant petty bourgeois dross houseroom.

The Decline in Union Membership, A Progressive Development?

"Many workers are on different levels aware that the unions are incapable of defending their interests ... Just look at the declining membership of unions. Workers aren't leaving or failing to join unions because they lack class consciousness. They see clearly that it is a waste of time and money joining an organisation that does not defend their interests."[31]

Of course the Tories tell it the other way round, the decline in union membership is due to a rejection of collectivism, the growth of conservative (selfish) values and a victory for Thatcherism. Both views are entirely wrong. In the first case that of the ACF, if workers were leaving unions, or not joining unions because of some new found class consciousness, we should see some evidence of *greater more radical more militant* class activity taking the place of those conservative unions which do "not defend their interests". Where is it?

Have we seen a rise in strike activity accompanying the decline of union membership? Not at all, in fact the decline in strike activity almost matches exactly the trend in membership. This is true for two reasons, firstly the industries with the highest union membership density (%) were also the industries with the greatest propensity to strike. Loss of members is quite literally loss of strikers and potential strikers.

---

30) This man named Sue, late of the RCP, one time Anarchist Workers Group, where acting as Marxist-Leninist computer bug he helped it crash, with an obsessive hatred of traditional working class images particularly northern ones, has a mental deviancy rather than a political position. Only Johnny Cash came close to analysing his problem in the song of the same name. More of Sue later.
31) *Organise*, 28, Anarchist Communist Federation.

On one level the fall in the number of unions and more importantly members can be traced to rising unemployment, especially in traditional, heavily organised trades. There has been a decline in source of employment which were traditionally strongly organised. The British coal industry has always accounted for the greatest number of strikes in the country. In 1969 the NUM had 297,000 members, today it has around 9,000. The number of strike days lost has obviously fallen dramatically. **However neither the loss of members nor the number of strike days lost is due to any disillusionment with the union** from either a right or left perspective. *INDEED THE FALL IN MEMBERSHIP IS DIRECTLY ATTRIBUTABLE TO THE EFFICIENCY OF THE UNION AS A CLASS WEAPON,* and the consequential blitz unleashed by the ruling class as a result. **Deliberate** targeting of the industry for run down in order to weaken their collective class enemy. A similar picture is true right across heavy proletarian industry; and it is far from fanciful to see here a deliberate design to close down the industrial centres with the most combative and class conscious working class traditions, the industrial red industry of Wales and Scotland, Liverpool, Tyneside, Birmingham and the East End of London. That the ACF can stand the world on its head and see the decline in union membership as a *progressive* step mystifies me.

Even as traditional industry and the proletarian unions have been cut to the bone and the whole nature of 'work' in Britain changed, workers have stuck to unions. The same period covered by the NUM's decline we find an equal and positive rise in membership of NUPE.

1969	1979	1986	
305.000	692,000	658,000*	*result of cuts in the health service

The pay and living conditions of workers in trade unions is in almost all cases higher than those in non unionised equivalent workplaces (As pointed out earlier some large firms are prepared to pay slightly over the union rate to keep the union out, this too is the influence of unionism). Yet if we take ACF's refracted logic and apply it to the growth of NUPE we would conclude that the rise in membership must be due to a lack of class consciousness, by workers who haven't realised it is progressive NOT to be in unions.

What is the reality? NUPE's expansion has included the recruitment of 'professional' nursing staff and ambulance personnel, porters labourers and all manner of public employee. The response of NUPE on a nationwide scale is of course mixed and contextual but all sectors have responded with growing militancy in recent times. Traditionally health service unions have had an aura of business unionism and professionalism given their vocational orientation, nonetheless they have responded vigorously in defence of the health service with militant union action and a growing political \ class consciousness.

Class combativity in the health Unions at the time of writing, and largely as a result of outright devastation upon the Health Service with the consequential impoverishment of patient care, that the Royal College of Nurses founded as a specific block *against* class and union action now ballots on ending its 40 year No Strike constitution. Similarly the Royal College of Midwives an association who for 100 years has never even contemplated the strike now is forced by social conditions and growing consciousness to debate ending the prohibition.

That this process is taking place within work organisation which have resisted even the name Trade Union shows inter alia the way organisational functions can change under the impact of social events and heightened consciousness and class combativity.

Whereas once upon a time bank employees in their black garb and stiff collars give the impression of privilege the reality of their working conditions have always been harsh and arbitrary. This had led a bold band of men and women in a banking union to persist to a point where the BIFU is virtually the industrial union of finance and banking, an odd profession to see stepping out in the ranks of labour but one which the conditions of their work and real class relationship has put them.

In general whilst heavy industry has been decimated 'white collar' employment has expanded, initially such workers were alienated from trade unionism which they seen as 'working class' while they themselves felt part of the middle or professional classes. However regimented office conditions, loss of professional status, alienating job routines have 'proletarianised' to some extent white collar work. Looking at vast open plan offices with workers sitting behind rows upon rows of consoles and word processors and telephones, one is at once put in mind of the shop floor, a clean well lit shop floor but a factory nonetheless. This has been an important feature in the growth of Trade Unionism in these areas particularly among women workers, who are in general the biggest area of union membership growth. The emergence of ASTMS has been important the merger with TASS in 1988 has given us the Manufacturing Science and Finance Union rationalising responses across that whole sector and bringing together 600,000 workers in a single white collar union, covering engineering. electronics, air transport, junior Drs, chemicals, shipping and many more. The class potential of such a union cannot be characterised by the scabs at Timex any more than the Nottingham blacklegs of the NUM in '84 can characterise the NUM.

Of course, there is the plain fact that wage labour is a *de-facto* recognition that capitalism is in existence, that workers needs must be employed in order to survive, and as such, to that extent only, have accepted albeit temporarily, waged work. It means also that workers fuel the exploitative process in a thousand different areas, from arms manufacture, & the armed forces to servicing Government and Council administrations, it means engaging in anti social toil in slaughter houses, in nuclear power-stations, it means sitting behind desks and offices in the Welfare 'Benefits' industry, it means being tied up with the 'wham bam thank you Mam' Health Service, all quite independent of the workers actual social and political orientation. Many class conscious workers will try and avoid the more blatantly exploitative areas of work, building war ships, being teachers or prison wardens, working in Benefit Offices, many more will feel driven by their own immediate needs to take the job first and either look for something more principled later or else work for the revolutionary transformation of society after work. One is never too surprised to find self declared 'revolutionary socialist' teachers, but Workers Power's Probation Officer came as a surprise even to me. One wonders if there are any card carrying members of the 'revolutionary left' on the other side of the riot shields, creatures which Militant call "workers in uniform"!

UNION ORGANISATION DOESN'T *PRESUPPOSE* A REVOLUTIONARY OR EVEN NEC-
ESSARILY CLASS CONSCIOUSNESS. The problem here, as elsewhere is NOT the organisational form, but the ideological level of understanding. Workerists will be well shocked, but it
is workers who make scabs, who make racist gangs and march on fascist parades, who put on
the soldiers uniform, prison warders uniforms, policemen's uniforms, being a worker, being in
or out of a union, living in a slum, or being unemployed and oppressed doesn't of itself
produce militant opposition or revolutionary action. Revolutionary consciousness above all,
organising within organisations with a revolutionary design, revolutionary propaganda and
a revolutionary intervention in the process of social conditions are also necessary.

After all the thesis advanced earlier about workers acting within mass organisations only
works if the mass, and the organisation are engaged in a progressive direction, the presence
of the other two without the latter, has given us The NSM, the UDA, & The UDM.

What I have tried to argue is that the shape of the organisation engaged in struggle isn't the
decisive factor, our own revolutionary cells and network's do not replace the workers, or
workers organisations such as Unions, our role is not to substitute ourselves for them; but to
assist in the development of combative class consciousness and be in assistance in the class
war which is already taking place. In much the way that the late *Subversive* group was itself
subverted by contact with the class, local ACF branches, with a more or less working class
composition and genuine contact with the class, start to shift their ground away from the
vulgar ANTI-UNION verbiage of their founders. Merseyside ACF group dipped in the fire of
the Dockers struggle, sets itself alongside the Tameside Strikers, and in their Summer 98
edition of *'Resistance'* set out a perspective not a kick in the arse different from main stream
Anarcho-Syndicalism. One can only hope such pro- working class tendencies within certain
generally northernish groups, begin to dominate the anti- working class petty bourgeois
leadership doon sooth.

Hunting down union power

In one sense it will seem a little strange addressing an extensive pamphlet to the subject of
Unions and strikes and industrial struggles, at a time of their furthest ebb and deepest fall
from utility by the class. The enemies of industrial struggle, of workplace organisation, or
Industrial Unionism and Syndicalism, however, find this the best time to drop from the trees
and start picking at the bones, believing the current fall in membership and utility of Unionism
and workplace organisation prove some long cherished dogma about the irrelevance of class
etc. Before such myths get blended into folk legend, now seems as good a time as any to take
it on. After all, during times of mass industrial unrest and workplace ferment, facts speak for
themselves, even if our cynics never quite understand the language.

The Tory government has targeted for extermination industrial action. Whole unions have
been virtually wiped out and bankrupted, whilst unofficial strikers are hit with court injunctions, threats fines and dismissals. The blacklist, alive and well in the 1930s, is back in the
gaffer's top draw. Actions which workers previously fell back on instead of strike action,

work to rules, over time 'bans' - simply not working any, sick days, gaan canny's, poor work, and generally acting the goat, are themselves treated <u>as</u> unlawful industrial action with the same penalties. The official warning followed by the sack, against a backdrop of mass unemployment and the blacklist, have rapidly closed off methods of resistance we have been able to employ even in the bad old days of the last century. Trying to recruit into unions, or get people to stay in unions in these circumstances is difficult in the extreme. Employers, with the Tory party and media press baron's home crowd in full voice, egg on employers to stand off even the most determined of strikes. The Miners, the Printers, Keeton's etc. As a result of laws stopping secondary action, *and more particularly workers with enough bottle in sufficient numbers to defy them.*

Once strongly soladaristic groups such as the docker's have been severely weakened, although as the courageous and principled stand of the Liverpool dockers shows, blood and class principles are thicker than water. The whole city dock labour force sacked for refusing to cross the picket line of their mates to get to their own work, just after Xmas with the lack of money starting to tell, a mass meeting massively turns down the offer of £20,000 each to buy off the action, more money than the men had seen in their lives, but not enough to dint their resolve. With 200 blacklegs imported from down south the ships are getting loaded, but with worldwide solidarity action at its height, they cruise the international dock front looking for a hiding hole to unload in. Yet despite the most determined resistance, the lack of practical solidarity *at home*, Official TGWU leadership working its bollocks off to call off the strike, Blair and New Labour sealing off international solidarity actions, and two years of bitter hardship finally brought them down.

Slow strangulation of the union itself, withdrawal of recognition, imposed and divisive pay settlements, ending of negotiations, time off for union duties, or office facilities, deliberately weaken the standing of the union, demoralise the workforce and give a warning that industrial action will be met with the most determined resistance in the most adverse of social and economic conditions. Against this backdrop, with a decline in traditionally strongly organised workplaces and the rise of casual, part time, service industries, asking someone to join a union for the first time means risking everything. It has been hard in the new work situation to prepare a fightback on even the most fundamental level of safety, sanitary and wage conditions. Of course, if you are "outside and against the union" anyway you won't see what the fuss is about.

OUTSIDE AND AGAINST THE UNIONS

(A communist response to Dave Douglass' text "Refracted Perspective")

A **Wildcat** Pamphlet

OUTSIDE AND AGAINST
THE WORKING CLASS
Wildcat

The inaccurate nature of Wildcat's major personal attacks upon me have been dealt with as I went along, perhaps they like ACF also copied them from elsewhere what is certain is that they never checked the facts, nor subsequently have deemed it necessary to correct the lies which they continue to hawk around leftist circles. Wildcat's 'technique' such as it is, is to set up a straw man and then knock it down again, you cant argue with it, but then why should you want to? This is backed up by cart loads of distortion, take their criticism of my analysis of the Orgreave tactic, my point is clearly made that is was the wrong place, too predictable, too inflexible and drew us away from more successful action. I publicly made these points at the time of the strike, and we fought for them inside the strike organisation and were to some extent successful in spreading and diversifying the action. See Pit Sense Versus The State.

"BUT" they say "he publicly supported it (and therefore encouraged participation in this defeat at the hands of the pigs)". It is a downright lie and anyone involved in that strike who knows the battle around tactics knows that to be true, ask any of the massed ranks of SWPers who thought Orgreave was a kind of Lourdes and with whom I had furious public battles. Of course we went, and why is only too obvious, our mates were taking on the state, our neighbours were battling it out toe to toe with armed police, it was not some academic exercise you could just abstain from, of course we went and we fought bloody hard, but we argued about the tactic when it was the right time to argue and that wasn't in the middle of cavalry charge. To compare this explanation of the situation WE were in, with "lefties who encourage workers to do things which they know are a load of crap -- like voting Labour and calling on the TUC to call a general strike" is thoroughly dishonest. Like the earlier personal distortion it can only work because they know their pamphlet will go to people who are totally ignorant of the actual situation.

"What Douglass doesn't talk about at all in his reminiscences of the 1984-85 Great Strike is the antagonism that existed between the union apparatus and the unofficial actions of the miners and others in the mining communities which he thinks are just extensions of the union." Pit Sense Versus the State is entirely about this feature. Indeed most of the questions they raise under this heading are answered in that book as are their eternal problems with identifying The Union. It wasn't the UNION which tried to discipline strikers for brick throwing, some branches particularly in the moderate North Yorkshire area were not as wild as their South Yorkshire branches and tried to cut tactics according to their moderate width, in South Yorkshire branches issued weapons and set up hits on scabs and lorry's etc. Both were features of The Union the battle for control over, against,free use of, tactics is fully described in the above book, but it was not a question of The Bureaucrats imposing moderation while The Miners sought unrestrained violence and sabotage, different branches, different areas different elements of the bureaucracy itself were present in both camps. The struggle around this issue was fought out on the streets as well as in heated mass meetings of the union it simply never was as straight forward as Wildcat wishes to rewrite the story now.

One thing which cannot be allowed to pass is the lie that money given to "union bureaucrats generally never reached strikers at all and certainly didn't reach those known to be trouble-makers." This is simply a variant on the MI5 Maxwell slush money story invented by the secret service and using the media to discredit the miners leaders and the union in general. On every count it has been proved to be a downright lie, the same is true on this occasion. Hardship money was evenly distributed through areas and women's support groups strictly on the basis on numbers, it was relayed to branches on the basis of food kitchens and membership rolls, your political point of view or views on prevailing tactics or whether you were a picket or not never came into the equation. If Wildcat is going to make a charge, that the leadership of the NUM did NOT distribute money sent to them to support the strikers, what do they say they did with it? Did they embezzle it, spend it themselves? This is just the charge Cook made in his now totally discredited Central TV Cook report, that Wildcat should chose to repeat it *without the slightest shred of proof* seriously must make you question the honesty of their intentions.

Throughout the spurious document the authors are forced time and again to illustrate action by Union Members in Union branches and often in Union Areas engaged in struggle with THE UNION only they just for shorthand call the former The Miners, and the bureaucrats The Union. Its the tale the way Cajo tells it I'm afraid and it simply will not do as an accurate assessment of what is going on. To be honest Wildcat tells us straight they aren't really interested in what is going on anyway, they don't want "alternatives" to Unions likewise "We are not interested in representing anybody but in building up groups and networks of activists who want to escalate the class war by whatever means are necessary." Well not really, if it takes place in unions "The links we develop between class struggle militants now will be useful when mass struggles do break out ... It should be clear from what we've said so far that this process can only take place **outside and against** the unions." (Wildcat) So where is this process? Where are the anti union class struggle militants? Where is the evidence of anything remotely to do with this distorted vision of an anti union workers movement that doesn't believe in mass assemblies, delegates or democracy? We suspect it is hiding behind the lump of grey matter in the collective head of Wildcat and nowhere else.

A SUITABLE CASE FOR
TREATMENT
... poisoned Analysis

A tiny splintereen from RCP which then gained 'Observer' status with Anarchist Workers Group. Much of 'the line' is still RCP vintage, like criticising Class War for failing to call for "victory to Iraq" in the Gulf war. Class War's perfectly principled slogan "NO WAR BUT THE CLASS WAR" is slagged off as "Liberal pacifism". So class war is liberal pacifism? Living Marxism the yuppie glossy RCP magazine is described as having "very radical ideas" one of which turned out to be support for the Countryside Alliance.

In reality Analysis is one strange man Susil Gupta with a word processor and too much time on his hands. Certain naive comrades within Class War have been courted by this individual to the point where they, at Class War's expense circulated the whole "Analysis" manifesto to every CW member and group in Britain. This manifesto by the way called for the dissolution of Class War. (My inbuilt paranoia makes me see this as a time bomb, a destructive seed circulated throughout the organisation and left to fester, ultimately to come to fruition, self criticisms and all, in Dec. '96. The March 22 ('97) meeting in Nottingham effectively laid the ground for a split between those like London and Doncaster Class War Groups who consider the organisation essentially sound and capable of continuing the struggle and the rest of the old Fed who wish to wind up and metamorphose as something else, time will tell, but I with the rest of Doncaster am sticking with the old brigade.) However, the seeds of destruction were planted or carried into the organisation's roots, at the time Gupta's view was quite plain.

Describing the illustrious team thus:- *"Left communists, political anarchists, life style anarchists, and 'I don't read books' anarchists, rebel's and ravers, intellectuals and stone throwers, dedicated revolutionaries and t shirt revolutionaries, localists and globalists, thinkers and beer drinkers ..."* Yep that sounds like us OK - but then he goes on, *"Trends which do not really belong in the same organisation"*. Is he crazy? What other organisation COULD we all fit into? Needless to say Sue is firmly in the 'I hate the Unions' camp, as they are "irrelevant". He seems to carry a particular hatred for the miners and Scargill, who, apart from staging his own arrest in '84, and doubtless his own assault as well, is described as "A wet paper bag".

Scargill "made up" the story about Colombian children working in coal mines, "to pluck middle class heart strings". But Colombian children DO WORK IN COAL MINES although it is not they nor the massive banks of modern machinery that allows coal to come to Britain cheaper than British coal, but a massive £40 per tonne state subsidy. "No quarter should be given to liberal romanticism about 'mining communities'. The job of a Yorkshire miner is no different from that of a dinner lady in Camden or a dustman in Glasgow. To wax lyrical about 'mining traditions' brass bands and pit communities only leads to an opportunist strategy based upon courting middle class liberal approval."

But we do live in close pit communities which have a shared sense of socialist and militant traditions, we do have a collective history and most have generations following on one from the other in continuous working histories underground with all that means in terms of a collective history of struggle going back decades and in some cases centuries. This may or may not sound "romantic" to Sue and the middle class colleagues he hates so much, but they remain facts. It just so happens that, yes, most pit villages also have at least one brass band; does that presuppose a strategy aimed at courting middle class approval? The dinner ladies job and that of the dustman in Glasgow are important to them as much as the miner's is to him, but the onslaught against the pit communities was an entirely political action and nothing to do with basic "market forces" or "uneconomic pits". Our arguments, aimed at showing that the mines were not in any terms "uneconomic", was not exclusive to economic rationalism, but in order to demonstrate the class politics of killing off the miners as a social force.

The Industrial Research and Information Service, an undercover right wing organisation set up in 1963 by Harold Macmillan, recruited right wing Union bosses to act as a fifth column within the ranks of labour. Nowhere was this more true than during our strike of '84-85. Steel workers leader Bill Sirs, Engineering Union leader Ken Cure and Wakefield District Council Leader, and one time NUM Branch Secretary have all been paid directors of the IRIS. David Osler, writing in the New Statesman tells us "Union leaders enjoyed substantial financial backing ... in return for their role in internal union machinations, with senior Tory peers acting as the link men". Bill Sirs was director of the IRIS during the miners' strike when a massive police and British Steel Corporation plan was laid to run coke from Orgreave to Scunthorpe steel mills, trying to block the fleets of scab trucks running through Britain's biggest most strike bound coalfield, became a major distraction from picketing elsewhere. It was in essence a second front opened by the enemy camp. "Another known IRIS director Ken Cure of the Amalgamated Engineering Union (AEU) sat on Labour's ruling National Executive Committee, during the entire dispute while Sirs was on the General Council of the TUC. Through these two men IRIS had access to the deliberations of the highest bodies of the labour movement, essential intelligence in the strike breaking effort against 'the enemy within'." IRIS was financed through tax deductible donations from dozens of Britain's biggest companies, in '64 it had been given a grant equivalent in today's terms to £500,000 from MI5.

Gupta could never accept any vision of the miners as a class vanguard, of course. In a personal letter to members of Class War after Heseltine's axe destroys all but ten or eleven mines in the whole of Britain, Sue is well pleased and announces that he is "glad the miners have been defeated".

"In a sense I am glad the miners have been defeated. If you crawl on your belly begging from the bourgeoisie then you deserve a good kick in the teeth."

In a review of my pamphlet Coal Communities in Conflict he quotes with glee the apparent "weakness" of my position. "Yes, there's been talk of industrial action, but the call for industrial action cannot be made on the abstract basis of "No job losses, No pit closures" the call has to be made for "No compulsory redundancies". If it's not to be compulsory, they'll have to put more money on the table for those who want out or else yes we'll take strike action and sink the few pits they do want to keep." In *"exposing Douglass's real position"* Gupta comments *"In other words Douglass accepts compulsory redundancies and just wants more money. The threat of "sinking" profitable mines is just bravura to cover up the tameness of this position. No miner in a profitable pit* will *allow it to be sabotaged."* Even a rational person might have difficulty understanding the situation from the outside, but when you are Moses, of course, it becomes impossible. The pamphlet was written a good 18 months before the Heseltine announcement and was a long term projection of possible government plans and how we might mobilise support for opposition. Read in this context the pamphlet was highly accurate in its predications especially the scale of the closures.

Following the defeat of the '84-85 strike periodic strikes had swept the collieries and coalfields. Management actions became more and more draconian with sackings, victimisation, court injunctions and writs. Anger gave way in many cases to an intolerable hatred of the job itself, "shut the bloody pit" was just as likely to be a response to management offensives as "strike". Gupta is quite wrong, many miners were quite prepared to sink ANY colliery, in order to get out, a number of highly profitable collieries WERE sabotaged to death in response to jackboot management. "No job losses" *in abstract* held no resonance for such men, they *wanted* job losses if it meant them getting out of an industry they had come to hate. Winning a strategy for 'no pit closures' when perhaps a majority of men at any pit would vote to shut it if the money was right, was not of itself going to mobilise the miners into strike or any other action. These are the facts of the situation we found ourselves in. How to address it? The redundo freaks, as we called them, only wanted out on the right terms, i.e. enough money. At the time of writing that pamphlet British Coal hadn't any enhanced redundancy terms on offer, which meant that if they were going to close collieries or get rid of men WITHOUT the bribe of big payoffs, they would have to bring in compulsory redundancies, in other words you'd be going out, but with nowt in your pocket. This is NOT what the redundo freaks wanted, and I reasoned a ballot call for strike action "against compulsory redundancies" would unite the men who wanted to save the jobs and the pits, with those who actually wanted out but on decent terms. Its seemed the only way on uniting an uneven constituency of miners.

The strategy was ultimately outflanked by the fact that payouts of up to £45,000 were later put on the table, however by that time we were building a mass of resistance to the closures themselves. What must be understood is that we hadn't until the launch of the much criticised public campaign convinced THE MINERS of the point of fighting, the men thought they were going to be on their own again and resolved that they wouldn't again fight alone. This is why we delayed for so long to get firstly the rail union RMT and to a lesser extent ASLEF on board, and then pointlessly as it turned out the GMB and the power workers. We wanted a united strike across the mines, rail and power stations, we delayed taking action because it was worth getting joint action if we could. We didn't succeed but still produced 12 million lost work days in two days of joint strike action and solidarity action by a number of workers unconnected with the mines or railway.

It is simply untrue to allege that the miners were straining at the leash for action and "Scargill" was holding them back to win public opinion. Scargill had to be held back from calling for action too early, that is before the mass of the members were convinced we could win. We always intended to strike and we always intended to try and spread the action, but we couldn't just do it because we wanted to; we had to convince others too and to large measure we failed. But it was never as Gupta says in this cockeyed passage: "Class War has the same approach as the NUM: avoidance of a *strategy* which can be the common basis for a wider working class movement - defence of jobs - in favour of tactics to keep the union together - more money for redundancy. I doubt that many CWers have noticed this because you are so unpolitical that you just don't see the political significance of anything." The fact is unless Sue has thought of it, it can't be a strategy.

Our strategy failed, that's not because we didn't have one but because we couldn't mobilise enough industrial action outside the mines. Clearly we did call for it long and hard. Sue's strategies will not fail, because they don't apply to anyone, they are just thoughts on paper and that's where they are condemned to stay, in Toon land. Talking of Toons, he picks up on another part of the pamphlet which rattles him: "I'll tell you this, they aint so strong. They're even shit scared of rave parties - never mind national strike action. Maybe we should adopt it as a new form of direct action. Rave for rebellion. Beats wandering round Birmingham on a wet Sunday with the same old worn out SWP chants. I urge Class War to adopt the mass rave as a weapon in the protest armoury. Anyway if we fail and they shut the pits there's a canny few pitmen have got their wigwams packed now. We're going to try some of this fresh air and freedom bit. We'll have some of that safe sex, drugs and rock and roll. I want to fornicate on some rich bastard's front lawn and have a shit in his wood." He asks in all seriousness, "Do you think that an organisation that puts out this kind of rubbish can really provide the working class with any leadership. Do you think that this will inspire any worker who has taken the decision to become a revolutionary?" Susie baby, its a joke! Its meant to be <u>funny</u>. The pamphlet is a verbatim copy of the speech I made at Class War's conference on Communities in Conflict. That weekend the papers had been full of reports of the hippies and travellers in the upper class rural heartlands of Britain; I thought I'd include a topical contemporary point. It was taken by the audience in the light hearted manner intended, but also as an act of solidarity with ravers and travellers who are facing discrimination. Incidentally a number of my mates from the pits <u>have</u> given up working and gone off with the New Agers (I made one the source of one of my songs, *The Young Redundant Miner,* a refrain from which goes: "So take ya job and shove it, take ya pit and shut it! I never liked the Bastard and hate the Bugger now, I'll live a life of leisure, in the fresh air at me pleasure, so Goodbye Mr Ainley coz I'm fuckin jackin in!). In a sense trying to explain working class attitudes and actions (let alone my songs) to Gupta is a waste of time when clearly he has little patience with either. As the old Yorkshire saying goes, "Yi can't educate pork".

Anti working class sentiment is rarely far beneath the verbiage of his literature:-
"Here is Dave Osler of Socialist reporting on the GEC Alsthom (formerly Ferguson Paillin) strike in January this year. His report is a good illustration of the conservative, stagnant and narrow attitudes that pervade shop-floor activism and provide almost all the clichés of Labourist romanticism; the golden glow of a mythical tradition, the "dignity of toil", "the

lads" "the empire" craftsmanship and deference to seniority. All that is missing is a brass band playing the theme music from the Hovis advert and a Northern accent, which the reader's imagination can provide." The strike is mainly about saying a flat "no" to 142 compulsory redundancies. On another level it is also about tradition, pride in a job well done and the right to have a bit of laugh while you work. "It was a bloody good firm when I came here 39 years ago" said Lenny, a picket in his sixties. "You worked hard but you enjoyed it ... Ferguson Paillin was world renowned. You could go anywhere in the world and find Ferguson Paillin switchgear. People used to have pride here. Now they just knock it out. I never thought this place would go like this ... You get a bloke been here a month telling a bloke who's been here 33 years he's not wanted." "You worked hard and you enjoyed it! This is the sort of backward subservient sentimental rubbish that prolonged exposure to trade unionism can cause ... It is obvious that when it comes to class struggle any wet behind the ears management trainee or sharp suited union official from head office can run circles round our Lenny, and Lenny is what grass-roots trade unionism is all about."[32]

In fact what is obvious from the contemptuous comments is that the working class, especially the northern working class, is hated by whoever inhabits the world of Analysis. Middle class intellectuals who feel alienated and ill at ease with working people find such comments very comforting, they don't actually have to like workers at all. You can despise everything they say and do, and still be a prophet of socialism. Would *ANY* worker in Britain tolerate the public expression of, let alone identify with, the following:- "Phelps Brown recognises well that trade unionism breeds that stupefying docility and spirit of compromise which the Establishment so admires in 'their' workmen." Britain in any case, we are told, "has no revolutionary tradition, Marxist or otherwise". "Of course, there is no such thing as a labour movement" either.

That we are being spoken to by some superior elite is characterised as much by the *manner* as the content of the criticism of the left for example *"The average lefty in Britain is a miseducated ill read moron who does not even read what his organisation produces."* Why can I hear Flashman from Tom Brown's schooldays when I read that sentence? But it gets worse the closer to working people Sue gets. Talking of the framed Winston Silcot, banged up in jail for an assassination he didn't commit, he says: *"He was a particularly nasty thug and a bully for whom settling class scores with the state was the last thing on his mind ... a lot of them named Silcot because he was universally considered a bad person ... criminal scum like him always scarper when the community gets involved in confrontations ..."* On SWP members: *"In reality a pool of lower level largely ignorant and inarticulate members always allows the leadership to isolate those who want to change it."*

---

32) The End Of Cowley Man, Analysis Winter 1992-93. If those of us are such dross, what is the extent that the vanguard elite will educate us? The vietcong, we are told, not only taught the peasants to read but also "to sing (!) to discuss films and learn about its history." Poor bastards eh? Didn't even know how to sing and discuss films before the vanguard arrived. Analysis in typical distorted vision can't see that the Vietcong for example actually grew FROM the history of peasantry and was composed BY them, not the other way round. If you tell it that way it follows that the revolutionary organisation and the direction of any particular struggle will come From a class conscious working class and not the other way round. This of course will leave no role for Sue.

The revived campaign to save the pits in '92 & '93 which led to the greatest public campaign in most people's lifetimes, and 12 million lost workdays in just two days of joint strike action, a mass civil disobedience campaign by Women Against Pit Closures which included occupations and blockades, is described as "a non event".

The contempt for working people is barely held in check: *"... the most important thing for the working class is its economic situation, but unfortunately it is prevented from doing anything about it because of ideological problems ..." "The traditional labourist working class, predominantly made up of older workers is hopelessly lost and will never recover. This section of workers the 'organised labour movement' is going to be crushed completely. Its only politics is to bleat for charity and mercy. On the other hand there is the new working class, younger workers in the 20-35 age group for whom labourism means nothing. Today their attitude is conservative and pragmatic ... They vote Conservative...because they are pragmatic, the Tories are the best people to run capitalism. Our hope lies in the latter section of workers ..."*[33]

So there we have it, not the organised working class who are washed out, certainly not the unions, not the strikers, not the women down at the pit camps or occupations, not black thugs, or ignorant malcontents - but young Tory voters! Not surprising that the contempt for the working class is mirrored by a strange respect for the rich: *"If British leftism was the hobby of the rich it would not be in the mess it is today because this class knows how to organise something grand and adventurous."* Certainly, like world poverty, war and destruction of the planet.

After quoting from The Guardian's "prospects for 1993" an unnamed South Wales miner talking about the favourable court judgement which had held that British Coal's arbitrary closure of ten of the threatened thirty one pits was illegal, and which had bought a temporary halt in the execution. Analysis concludes nothing of the human suffering engendered by this whole final bloody process and instead believes the miner to be imbued with contaminating middle class <u>sentiment</u>. "Before a stable revolutionary trend can be built within the working class <u>it must be cleansed</u> of every bourgeois and radical middle class idea, the miners 'non strike' has made it patently clear that what is left of the traditional labour movement is now totally swamped by middle class conceptions" (my emphasis). It must be cleansed? Does that sound like revolutionary Marxism, anarchism, or can we hear a distant echo of Pol Pot in there somewhere? He goes on, "Those of us that defend a revolutionary and independent working class line, will have to CREATE A PROLETARIAN INTELLIGENTSIA" (my emphasis) THEY will have to create a proletarian intelligentsia, taken with notions of "cleansing the working class" and their elitist notion of *15 to 20 dedicated people becoming the national revolutionary vanguard* doubtless drawn from the ranks of young Tory voters - given the obnoxious contempt for working people evident in all the documents under the Analysis heading, I should say we have here a wilfully anti-working class tendency whose trajectory could take it literally ANYWHERE, including deep into right wing political notions.

---

33) Most of the observations on Analysis come from the article The Passing Of An Old Warrior as does this quote, others from various copies of Analysis and correspondence between CW members and Sue Gupta, all documents in my possession.

Hardly surprising that given the perspective of Heavy Stuff 5 (charge of the left brigade) with its refutation of left vanguards and revolutionary elites that Sue has launched a personal attack upon me.

After all he places his own 'organisation' above the class itself, when one reflect on what this 'organisation' actually consists of, it shows what base regard the working class itself is held in. "Every revolutionary puts his or her organisation first because no one can build a revolutionary organisation without believing its leadership is crucial to the working class."

There we have it, the dogma that sits at the heart of every degenerated revolution and movement, the self inflated leadership which robs the class of its direct independent rule and action. That Analysis is Leninist is always self evident but its talk of supremacy of 'the party', 'the cadre', 'the leadership', and the conclusion that "the working class needs good dedicated leaders", and knowing the people and movements they have contempt for, one can seriously ponder WHAT ELSE is coming. Under the heading "Party Patriotism" they claim "any revolutionary" puts their own organisation first - that is, before the class itself - in fact the working class is a docile flock of sheep gently grazing the pasture while the revolutionary leaders decide where we shall be herded to next. More, there is one part of this article which suggests that the working class can be dispensed with altogether, and this is the "advice" offered to Class War, which it seems is doomed: "its easy going radicalism had proved no match for what the bourgeois is throwing up ... so Class War can only now do what the rest of the left does - go with the flow and mark time - and become a parody of itself." and "Our assessment is that CW is now not only moribund, but that it is increasingly dominated by radical petit bourgeois ideas." Euthanasia is the kind suggestion: "Our advice to Class War members is that they should make a conscious decision to disband the organisation in an orderly and political way, and understand the political necessity of doing so".

So what's the big plan Analysis is sitting on? To "Acquire a comprehensive view of society to the extent that you have an intimate knowledge of the beast ..." "WE CONSIDER THAT THIS FIRST STAGE ALONE WILL TAKE A DECADE." Ten years to gather more academic bumf on 'the beast' that we don't already know, while we the working class sheep carry on grazing quietly until the carefully constructed intelligentsia, having gathered more 'input' than K9, emerges from its past Tory voting cocoon to round us up and offer us leadership. What about right now? "We think that in the absence of a revolutionary or even radical current within the working class THERE IS NO PRACTICAL SOLUTION TO THESE PROBLEMS" (my emphasis). That's right, go and have a nice lie down for ten years, you obviously need the rest. For my part I agree with what the Black Panther guy said "In my view the shit has been analysed and reanalysed enough, what's required is to get rid of it." Certainly nothing Analysis can offer anybody will be of assistance in fighting for the next round of drinks let alone a revolutionary transformation of society, there must be serious concern at the unstable and very questionable 'ideas' advanced by this man and his paper. What is curious is that even middle class anarchists should tolerate him.[34]

---

34) Most of the observations on Analysis come from the article The Passing Of An Old Warrior, copies of Analysis and correspondence between CW members and Sue Gupta. All documents are in my possession.

Unions Progressive &/or Revolutionary?

The reality of the wage labour relationship is as previously stated one which is *inherently* conflictual, and while the dominant ideology of a union may influence the way in which the situation is dealt with in relation to the predominant social conditions of the period, the class contradictions will remain unresolved. 'Traditional' Unions in fact, almost despite themselves, challenge the 'rate of exploitation' and implicitly 'the rights' of capital over labour. However there is nothing of itself in a union to prevent it becoming an instrument for revolutionary class struggle.

Some unions such as the NUM not only have a constitutional aim of overthrowing capitalism they have also at times ideologically and practically challenged its existence. Unions particularly with a more democratic base and mass membership involvement, with active workplace branches, shop stewards and shop floor assemblies are ideal units of working class resistance not necessarily restricted to immediate bread and butter issues but for raising questions of the tasks for class war in general.

Marx argued that there is a dialectical interaction between capitalist society and trade unions, with both revolutionary and conservative elements present at the same time, some of that has been illustrated in this pamphlet.

Prior to the 1917 Russian revolution it could be said that Chicago rather than Petrograd was the world inspirational centre of revolutionary action, particularly after 1905 and the foundation of The Industrial Workers of The World.

The IWW had set <u>the working class itself</u> centre stage, their self action, their direct control of organisation would carry through the revolutionary overthrow of capitalism and BE the basic infrastructure of the alternative society emerging at the other side. This was the popular conception amongst the Marxist supporters of the IWW (the SLP for example) as well as the Anarchists.

However following the Russian revolution Lenin and the Bolsheviks, because they seemed to have actually put theory into practice and delivered the goods, developed as the world leadership of the 'revolutionary movement'. Lenin despite the perfectly correct slogan of "All power to the Soviets" (i.e. the democratic workers and soldiers committees) set <u>The Party</u> centre stage, particularly after 1921. Henceforth all features of working class struggle were subservient to The Party which was deemed to be the living manifestation of 'the workers' and their cause. He declared that the best Unions could do was develop 'Trade Union Consciousness'. Only The Party could actually organise a revolution. Lenin's view is essentially a petit bourgeois position, but the fact is, it changed the way in which the newly emerging communist movement regarded unions and workers self activity independent of 'The Party'. This change has put a stamp on much of the left, even the non-Leninist left's view of unions and union struggles. Marxists retaining the earlier (non-Leninist) views were usually thereafter (wrongly) described as Syndicalists (people like Jim Larkin, James Connolly for example). The rendering of workers in their own organisations to be inferior to the external 'revolutionary' body is <u>not</u> because of say inferior 'Trade' Union weaknesses over the IWW for example, this perception would see the IWW and organisations like them as inferior also. It is a concept which holds that ONLY the external 'revolutionary' body can develop a total political class perspective. It is a concept in direct opposition to my own view of class struggle and the revolutionary potential of the working class, even when in constricted organisational forms such as Trade Unions.

What is at first sight surprising is that a number of self declared Anarchists should take up the Leninist critique of the limitations of trade unions and turned it into a declaration of war against unions, in the process substituting Lenin's central place for 'The Party' with either some notional 'autonomous workers movement' or their own Simon Pure Revolutionary Anarchist Outlook. The idea when looking at class struggle is not however who can get the prize for the best alternative to things as they are, the most revolutionary form of class organisation we can imagine, *but how to engage into the struggle which is actually happening.* Take for granted most unions have suffocatingly parasitic bureaucracies, this does not render null and void the life and death struggles by working people engaging in Unions who in any case refuse to allow the bureaucracy to stifle their efforts. The struggle within Unions is also a struggle against right wing bureaucrats, to clip their privileges, to pay only for days work undertaken on no more than the average wage of the workers they represent, to call them to account, in regular election and subject to immediate dismissal, for democratic rank and file control based upon branches, shop stewards groups of mass shop floor assemblies or office forums. Unions, or, more directly, the workers who comprise them, are open to posing political demands across the frontiers of trade and class conflict as a whole, they are open to debate and the adoption of revolutionary concepts for the transformation of society.

Goodbye To Unions?
O.K. Goodbye, but where are you going?

So almost full circle we come to "A Controversy About Autonomous Class Struggle In Great Britain" which is the response to my original critique of Cajo Brendel's pamphlet by that name, and is published in *Echanges Et Mouvement*. In this though another voice is joined that of Theo Sander, adding his "Rise and Decline Of The Shop Stewards Movement As a Mediating Force".

Rise and Decline theories have been popular from time to time, the End Of Shop Stewards, and its big brother The End Of Trade Unionism, The End of Ideology and even at a time "The End Of The Working Class" and Class Struggle itself! The facts are as outlined earlier in this pamphlet related to the destruction of heavy industry in Britain, the planned growth of unemployment as a whip against militancy, anti union legislation and more importantly a widespread feeling of demoralisation in the *perception* of power in the working class. This is reflected in a loss of class combativety previously seen in the powerful shop stewards movements on the shop floor, especially of the giant car plants.[35] Theo it seems is such an expert on the subject he is inclined to invent "shop stewards" for the mining industry, something we have never ever had. Union structure in the coal industry are quite different,

and he ought to know since clearly he has systematically trawled my work looking for hooks to hang criticisms on. Some of these have been dealt with in the course of the text, his placing me in a position of NUM branch leadership a decade before I was actually even running for a position, his mockery of my 20 year old analysis of the role of the Labour Left in the period and for some reason his amusement at my terming democratic unofficial assemblies of the NUM branches "quasi soviets". A "Soviet" after all is a workers committee or council. The fact is the unofficial movement of 1969 in the coal industry, highly in tune with the progressive trends and tendencies of the period all over the world did impact within our Union and ousted old moderate leaderships and constitutions setting the scene for highly important battles of 72 & 74. His comrade Cajo quotes more than once from the militant period in general and miners in particular. Just why Theo should not "have any particular reason at all to let ourselves be carried away like that by memories of a past that never was."

I am at a loss to understand, does he suggest there was NO unofficial movement? That we didn't launch in 1969 a massive unofficial nationwide strike, the first in 40 years? That this WASN?T organised by rank and file militants heavily leaning toward left labour and revolutionary politics against conservative moderate leaderships which had dominated the union since the end of world war two? That constitutional changes (for example the strike vote requirements) and Branch level leadership changes reflecting the different complexion and combativety of the members *DIDN'T TAKE PLACE?* That this process *didn't* clear the way for the actions of '72 and '74? "A Past That Never Was"? What? Just because you don't believe it? I confess to being used to debating facts, yes the meaning of historic events too, as we shall turn to next, but around the centrality of 1969 in the developing movement, I see no grounds for its refutation and frankly none are offered.

The central theme of Sanders polemic is the nature of Nationalisation of the coal industry, and the astonishing statement *"No, under nationalisation it wasn't the same as before, in every possible respect it was infinitely worse than anything miners had suffered from private coal owners".*[36] We are not here talking of some far off distant period of history which is now so far off we might only speculate about it, many many retired miners and their wives fully recall their lives under private ownership and the contrasts of the years of Nationalisation. The miners of my generation were raised by parents and grandparents all of whom had laboured under "The Masters", as they were known. Theo, we have no need to speculate or bandy statistics ASK the miners, their answers will be unanimous and unequivocal. To show Theo's

---

35) Ironically a little after penning their Goodbye To Unions, general strikes rocked Spain Italy and France, while MG Metal Germany's biggest Union launched its mass strike programme and British Rail's network came to a total shut down three times in less than two years and millions upon millions of European workers behind their various Union banners demonstrated that although weakened, they had not gone away. I have included examples as I have gone along and almost as they occurred in the course of writing the pamphlet, these examples are far from comprehensive.
36) Theo Sander, The Rise and Decline Of The Shop Stewards Movement As A Mediating Force, in Goodbye To The Unions, Echanges Et Mouvement, p38.

statement to such folk is to invite disbelief and ridicule.

The reign of slaughter which was the reality of private coalownership is well documented, not least by the countless mass graves which mark our grave-yards and serried ranks of tombstones the victims gone to gas and water inundation, explosion, rock fall and dust. Look then at the names on the stones and their ages, children of five, up to grandads of seventy, all with the same name, whole families blown away or sealed in concrete tombs. Look to the tributes to the union fighters against "The Bond" that contract which in Scotland tied all male children from the day of their birth to the ownership of the mineowner along with the man himself, who threatened the child, the parents and any employer with jail should they seek to engage them, or spirit them away. In Northumberland and Durham the bond was yearly and a bloody struggle often with arms in hand was waged by the early union members and their families. The coal counties of Britain were as separate countries with a mass diversity of terms and conditions and different wage rates and union strengths and weaknesses. A united strike in one county had seen the importation of unemployed and impoverished miners from another. Coal Owners could trade off one set of coal miners against another and manipulate strikes and lock-outs as the market for coal suited. There was no pension rights, no early retirement, no redundancy payments, no social security, or dole, you worked till you dropped. "Nationalisation, *infinitely* worse than anything the miners had suffered from private coal owners" its a poor jest Theo.

In terms of conditions the pits were cauldrons of hell. The owners though opulent in their life styles kept investment in machinery to the minimum, the strength of a mans back and the power of his arms was cheap and disposable, machines were neither. In the southern coalfields women and young girls did the work of the ponies in the northern fields, again because they were cheaper. Indeed it was often noted that after an explosion the owners asked first "how many ponies were killed?" since they were more expensive than the colliers lives. Shallow seams and narrow seams usually more dangerous than deeper and thicker seams were worked because they were more accessible and required less capital. In short the pits were heavily labour intensive, and that is the main reason for the size of the workforce prior to nationalisation. Far more tonnage's were extracted under the latter with far fewer men because of the increasing capital investment made available by the state, which would never have been forthcoming under the owners.

It is true this cost jobs but it also allowed for negotiating more favourable retirement terms, it reduced the numbers of people, proportionately in the mine exposed to the most dangerous types of work. Had this been a truly socialist measure of course we should have kept the total volume of workers PLUS the machinery and allowed them to share out the work to two days per week for a full weeks pay. This wasn't socialism however, nobody suggests it was. It had been the barbaric conditions under the old masters which led the miners as a whole to become so militant and times revolutionary.

The miners were not hapless victims, they were among the first workers in Britain to organise unions, they fought back with strikes, riot, armed risings, and sabotage. In some places they won extensive inroads into the 'management prerogative' and instituted large areas of job control, particularly in terms of manning, but the life of the miner was often cruel and short. They also appreciated the ebbs and flows of industrial militancy and bargaining power, and sought to draft into law safeguards on minimum age, hours and health and safety, since they had learned from experience that a victory today could be taken away tomorrow, they hoped that widespread social upheaval would lead to regulatory laws which would be a more permanent restraint on the individual greed of owners, and looked to Workers Control of the mining industry and the overall abolition of capitalism and its replacement by socialism.[37]

Nationalisation in the form the post war labour Government introduced it, was not the "New Dawn" the miners had looked to for so long, but it *WAS* symptomatic of the strength of the working class that they were obliged to get rid of the owners (albeit with generous compensation) they standardised wage negotiation, centralised the workforce into a single body with a common enemy. They were forced to concede sweeping safety legislation and union recognition. The Corporations obligation to maintain health, safety and welfare were written into the 1946 Nationalisation Act. Eight years later the strongest most extensive piece of mine safety legislation to be passed *ANYWHERE* in the world, the 1954 Mines and Quarries Act was engaged ensuring that British mines would become the safest in the world (That is not of course to say they were *SAFE* far from it). This in turn led the way for improvements in hours, retirement ages, and training, none of these things together with wages were of course "settled" and if Theo, is trying to suggest that Nationalisation "softened" the miners or made them less militant he is again completely wrong, strikes, rag-ups and major disputes followed year on year as the figures clearly tell :-

---

37) The word "Socialism" is quite modern earlier periods seen workers using,less familiar designations, "A workers commonwealth" or "When all will be made level" the meanings were much the same, the common ownership of the means of production and exchange and the common ownership of wealth, land and power.

Year	Number Of Stoppages Starting That Year	Year	Number Of Stoppages Starting That Year
1900	120	1950	860
1905	82	1951	1,050
1910	209	1952	1,221
1915	79	1953	1,312
1920	213	1954	1,464
1925	164	1955	1,783
1930	150	1956	2,076
1935	217	1957	2,224
1940	318	1958	1,963
1945	1,306		

To recognise that Nationalisation was a massive improvement on the multitude of private owners doesn't mean we had established social harmony or a common goal or a joint enterprise, no we were still very much in the class war and we have fought it almost to a standstill over the last ferocious 24 years to the point of our near total extinction. I have personally suffered under the N.C.B. and British Coal, been victimised underground, blacklisted more than once, served High Court writs and summonses, charged with illegally stopping the mines, threatened with bankruptcy for the loss of millions of tonnes of coal,[38] threatened with eviction and the sack, been beaten and imprisoned fighting coal board bosses and their state, and now am unemployed and blacklisted from hell to breakfast time and face the rest of life in forced poverty. NOBODY needs try and tell ME the nature of nationalised bosses. But it is untrue, and wilfully untrue to say they are worse, never mind infinitely worse, than the Coal Owners, *especially* in terms of Health and Safety.

The Mines Inspectorate report for 1966 shows clearly the comparison between pre and post nationalisation e.g. fatal accidents between 1903-1912 were 1.33 whereas in 1955 it was 0.58. Serious accidents also show a marked decline, the same is even more dramatically true of the incidence of fatal and crippling lung diseases. The incidence began to drop dramatically after nationalisation, twelve years into the new N.C.B. it remained at more than 1 in 10 (11.2%) but had fallen to less than 1 in 100 (0.6%) by 1986. Theo had looked at the numbers of *"all accidents"* which does mark an increase, although clearly he doesn't know why. The fact is these are accidents which do not require time off work, or those which don't keep you off more than three days at which point they are classed as Serious Reportable Accidents. The simple facts are a) These accidents were firstly *never recorded* before under the reign of the owners, and then later if they were it was only because a workmen or a deputy had made a point of reporting it. So firstly not at all, and then very sporadically. b) The Union had not developed its strength and legal expertise to the point where it could claim compensation for accidents from which you had no time off work. In this situation, to the workman there didn't seem much point reporting them. Later we became very skilled at the recovery of damages even for accidents from which you lost no time, and for which there was nothing whatever to show you had had one. Men carried a sort of mental ready-reckoner scale, a black nail was

---

38) We always said it wasn't "lost" anyway, we knew where it was.

good for £50, a derailment from which your back was shook up, and for which you stopped off the next day, could be worth between £150 and £200. I became so expert at recovering damages for manriding trains jumping the tracks that many men were receiving more in compensation than they earned for a whole week's work.

The men referred to the obliging track as "Golden Rail" the gaffer's were baffled why Friday's night shift suffered more derailments than any other time, the men put it down to "metal fatigue". At other times a man might report a slight accident in order to keep a genuine excuse for being off work at a later period, perhaps during the kids holidays, more seriously men knew a little silly incident could in later years develop into serious medical consequences. All of which meant the work force was highly diligent in reporting slight accidents and in getting the deputy to issue a receipt of the report (an AR1 form) as evidence for future claims. None of this happened in the days of private ownership, that doesn't of course mean "all accidents" or the three days type weren't happening, only that they were not reported. It requires very little logic to appreciate that the numbers of deaths and serious accidents would be unlikely to fall so dramatically if the numbers of small accidents were independently rising at such a phenomenal rate, the actual trends are closely related, the incident which causes the slight accident is only a wee shove from a serious accident and the serious accident is only a slightly harder push to a death. How else can the figures be explained? Again nothing is offered to do so.

General Summary for Coal Mines Report H.M.I. Mines and Quarries 1966

(N/A = Not Available -- actually not recorded)

Year	No. of Persons Employed 1,000s	No.of Persons Killed Annually	No.of Serious Reportable Accidents	Deaths	RATES PER 1,000 PERSONS	
					Serious Reportable Accidents	Total Number
(Yearly Averages)						
1853-62	259.90	1,012	N/A	3.90	N/A	N/A
1863-72	340.80	1,069	N/A	3.14	N/A	N/A
1873-82	503.40	1,129	N/A	2.24	N/A	N/A
1893-1902	571.70	1,032	N/A	1.81	N/A	N/A
1903-12	957.80	1,275	5,729	1.33	5.50	148.10
1913-22	1,085.50	1,298	4,692	1.20	4.20	130.70

Year	No. of Persons Employed 1,000s	No.of Persons Killed Annually	No.of Serious Reportable Accidents	RATES PER 1,000 PERSONS		
				Deaths	Serious Reportable Accidents	Total Number
(Yearly Averages)						
1923-32	1,019.50	1,064	4,197	1.04	4.10	166.80
1933-42	777.00	877	3,123	1.13	4.00	181.30
1943-52	732.30	538	2,293	0.73	3.10	270.90
(Yearly Actuals)						
1955-56	725.90	328	1,452	0.45	2.00	302.80
1958	722.80	327	1,752	0.45	2.40	288.60
1959	688.00	348	1,676	0.51	2.40	306.00
1960	622.40	317	1,573	0.51	2.50	311.90
1961	589.90	235	1,477	0.40	2.50	320.60
1962	596.60	257	1,557	0.45	2.70	350.80
1963	542.00	254	1,402	0.47	2.60	377.60
1964	515.60	198	1,329	0.38	2.60	386.90
1965	484.60	216	1,159	0.45	2.40	428.90
1966	444.70	160	1,061	0.36	2.40	419.50

A Spread of Later Statistics

Labour Research Dept, March 1988

Year	No. of Miners	Deaths	Serious Injuries
1980-81	229,800	42	512
1981-82	218,500	35	815
1982-83	207,600	38	865
1983-84	191,500	30	824
1984-85	175,400	22	378
1985-86	154,600	28	715
1986-87	125,400	15	952
1987-88	104,400	9	729
1988-89	87,905	11	388

"There was a steady fall decline in the number of deaths and serious injuries to miners from Nationalisation in 1947 to 1976-77. In 1930, 1,013 miners were killed and 4,197 seriously injured but by 1979 this figure had reduced to 46 killed and 473 seriously injured. Although total employment had also fallen from 943,442 to 234,900 the decline in death and serious injury was significant especially since the nationalisation of the industry in 1947" (Table extracts from annual reports of Mines Inspectorate, quotation Labour Research Dept, March 1988 p4 Hazards Of Mining).

Private Mine Safety

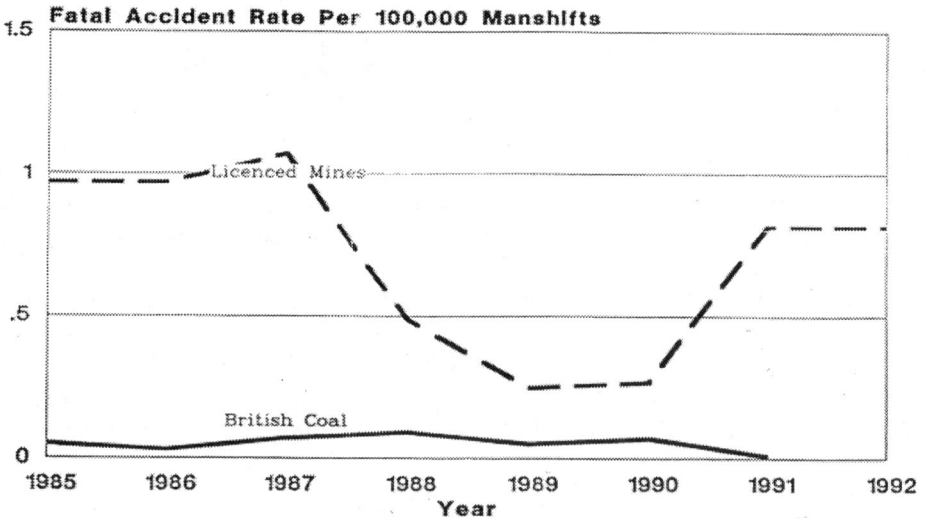

Fatal Accident Rate Per 100,000 Manshifts — chart showing Licenced Mines and British Coal, Years 1985 to 1992, rates from 0 to 1.5.

Neither can it be suggested that it is simply the passage of time which secured the increase in safety standards, private ownership methods were primitive while the nationalised industries were increasingly modern. Were this to be the case modern privately owned mines in South Africa or North America, Columbia or Europe *or anywhere* in the world would have better safety standards, lower death and serious injury rates than what Theo calls are the "infinitely worse" conditions under Britain's nationalised mines. In fact the next best to Britain's record pro rata to manpower is 50% more dangerous. If we care to look at South Africa we find a carnage in 700 miners killed every year, just in gold mining with a similar rate in coal mines. The United States has a death and serious injury rate 2/3rds in excess of Britain. But we have another test we can make, there are privately owned mines and private contract operations in Britain how do they compare to their nationalised counterparts, this is surely a *direct* comparison.?

On 4th Oct. 1988 *The Independent* revealed that accident rates in private deep mines were more than three times higher than those of British Coal. Out of an estimated work force of 1,800 three miners were killed at work in both 1986-87 and 1987-88 and 15 in 1985-87. "In other words the risk of dying in a private coal mine is 1 *in* 600 a year in comparison with 1 *in* 10,000 in British Coal's mines"[39]

---

39) The Hazards of Coal Mining LRD March 1989 p19

By 1988 more than 10,000 private contractors were working in the mining industry under the employ of private mining firms (this was the prelude to the full scale privatisation of what remained in 1994). These workers accident rates were almost double that of British Coals direct labour 5.31 as compared to 2.97 per 100,000 employees. Whereas British Coal's employees enjoying stronger union rights and employment protection regularly reported accidents even of a most minor nature for the various reasons explained, the contractors with no employment rights, weaker union protection and 'fire at will' bosses refused to report even serious accidents for fear of the sack. Peter McNestry of NACODs told LRD of one his deputies who "recently found a contractor's employee working with three broken fingers. As he could not have put on his self rescue equipment alone, he was both a danger to himself and to other workers. But he refused to report the accident as this would have meant the sack."[40]

Wages following the end of the strike continued to improve due to skilful contract negotiations, blocking management attempts to impose unfavourable contracts, and workers holding onto their independent job control and control over overtime, and week-end work allocation. These were important frontiers of control, and allowed for earnings in excess of £20,000 per year for many workers not simply those on the face but in outbye and surface operations such as material transfer and transport. Face workers regularly earned in excess of £15000 per year without overtime.

To try and compare this to the earnings of outside, private companies or to look for hard areas of independent job control in firms with cavalier hire and fire attitudes is frankly laughable, *there is no comparison.*

Theo's position *"No, under nationalisation it wasn't the same as before, in every possible respect it was infinitely worse than anything miners had suffered from private owners.* The NCB was definitely not the weakest enemy, not the least oppressive, not the one on which the union could direct more pressure and obstruction. on all counts *the exact opposite is true* although it is perfectly correct to say that the NUM has permanently acted as if it is wasn't." (my emphasis).[41] This is not simply *untrue* it is a gross distortion of the facts. Of his comment "The NUM has *permanently* acted as if it wasn't" what are we to make? That the NUM hasn't fought the NCB? That under the NCB there have been fewer strikes than under the owners? The figures as illustrated in this text prove that this assertion is entirely without substance to back it up.

Recently we have seen the wholesale privatisation of the coal industry in Britain and with it has returned some of the worse excesses of the dark days (or should we say *darker* days) before nationalisation. At Hatfield (from which I am now blacklisted along with all other union officials and activists of the NUM) privatised since Feb. 94 there have been no safety inspections under s123 of the M&Q A.[42] Now there is no problem over "all accidents" reportage

40) ibid. p18
41) Theo Sander, in Goodbye To The Unions, Echanges Et Mouvement, p38
42) Section 123 of the Mines & Quarries Act gives workmen the *independent* right to inspect the whole mine without management interference, and to report directly to the government Mines Inspectorate. It

because the rule is if anyone reports more than three of these minor accidents they are automatically sacked. A worker who broke his arm was sacked as he lay on the medical centre floor on a stretcher. An overman on whom an iron door collapsed,breaking his leg, was told his wages would be paid while off work so long as the accident (a serious reportable) wasn't reported. The man bathed and taken home, then an ambulance phoned for, transported to hospital claimed to have fallen over his dog whilst at home. A surface material worker had his hand run over by a tub was carried *past* the medical centre and taken to a distant hospital in order to avoid the management's practice of phoning the local hospital to see if any miners from his pit had reported there, so they could be disciplined or sacked. So we shall see in the accident statistics still more 'proof' for Mr Sander's strange theory, that the privatised Hatfield Colliery has *no* minor accidents and very few serious accidents, in contrast to the floods of reports under the nationalised Hatfield. Theo's figures with no one to guide him will *prove* the private mine to be safer than the nationalised mine, but it won't *actually* be true any more than the former comparison was.

Big rise in serious mining accidents

Workface/ NUM anger as figures reveal 'legacy of privatisation', reports Seamus Milne

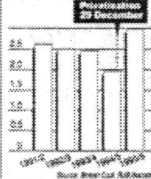

Heated debate . . . Miner Phil Thatcher demands fair deal for coal at a Commons lobby yesterday

Wages at the colliery are about the same as before, except that they are linked to meeting a weekly production target, failure to do so means men having to stop FOR NO ADDED WAGES until it is reached, even if it means working Saturday and Sunday FOR NOTHING AT ALL! Previously they would have had wages at time plus a half, and double time. A ten hour shift frequently replaces the 7-1/4 hour shift for no added wages. Contracts such as they are are no longer negotiated they are imposed, take it or leave it and the blacklist rules supreme.

It has taken some time for the Mines Inspectorate to get the wool from over its eyes but even they have become disturbed by clear trends of figures being falsified, and accidents being unreported and hidden. "1997 is the worse year of the decade with a major accident rate of 3.9 per 100,000 Manshifts and dangerous incidents 200% up" Mr R Stevenson Principle Mines District Inspector of Mines. 16. Feb. 98.

was a right closely guarded in the nationalised mining industry, but until recent union campaigns to reverse the trend, under fear of the sack it collapsed into total disuse in many private mines.

The Pit However Is Still The Pit. NCB / British Coal Mines Were Not "SAFE"

For fear of further distortion let it be stated with absolute clarity although the nationalised industry was _safer_ than conditions endured by miners under private ownership this does not mean to say they were SAFE as such.

Miners still got killed and injured in the most horrific manner. Theo will be aware of this because he has read my book _A Miners Life_ which clearly spells out working conditions in British Nationalised mines and the hazards we (and that includes me) had to face working them.[43] We of all people as life long miners actually _working_ in these conditions know the limitations on health and safety at work even in nationalised industries too (I am aware Theo thinks local pit Union officials don't actually work down the mine in hazardous conditions and anti-social shifts, but this is just another of his grossly inaccurate assumptions).[44]

"Health and Safety Executive (HSE) accident statistics published in Oct. 1988 showed that coal mining remains the most dangerous industry in which to work; more dangerous even than construction. As the report notes "The rate of accidents and major fatal injuries (per 100,00 employees) in 1985 for coal extraction etc., is over three times the average for manufacturing and 1.3 times that for construction. These ratios are even higher for coal mining by itself (4.6 and 1.8 respectively)"[45] "By 1987-88 non-fatal major injuries in coal mining were 2.7 times those of construction".[46]

Frontiers Of Control

Safety at work, wages, conditions, shift patterns etc. are frontiers in the class war in the work place. It is a frontier which is pushed one way and another according to the strength and bargaining power of each respective side. That we started to slip back in our steady improvements since nationalisation in 1947 came as a result of concentrated countervailing class forces in a deliberate action. One of the unifying elements in the industry and one which

---

43) Earlier I had written The Slaughter Of The Miners By The NCB (published by Socialist Union Press and available on the inter-library loan service) does that title suggest to _anyone_ that I considered the NCB as a "safe" employer? Before that The Need For Workers Control In The Mining Industry (Published by 1Vth International Publications, same source).

44) It might be worth stating that had Theo been making a point about Soviet nationalised mines in contrast to say German private mines he might have had a point as it is Both are far more dangerous and potentially fatal than British Nationalised mines.

45) The Hazards of Coal Mining, Labour Research Dept, March 1989 Health and Safety Executive Report Oct. 1988.

46) The Hazards of Mining p4

drafted the divergent counties into a single workforce had been the development of a national day wage system. It had abolished local piece rates and a multitude of price rates, abolished the evil of contract work which paid more for more coal filled and fired. A system which had made young men old and broke strong backs in a effort to keep a high income. The day wage paid all similarly graded workers the same rate wherever they worked and whatever production or lack of it they achieved. This stopped men literally killing themselves to get more cash, and also gave the same interest in national negotiations with the employer, the NCB. The development of this National Power Loading Agreement undoubtedly was a key strategic factor in bringing about the successful national actions of '72 and '74. For this reason the incoming Labour Government resolved to get rid of it, to break up the unifying factor, to create divisions between the various counties once more. Over the top of conference decisions, NEC decisions and two national ballots they introduced the Incentive Scheme. Its divisive effect came to bare fruit in '84-85 when the more prosperous and protected Nottingham and Midlands coalfields decided to ignore the struggles of their less rewarded northern and Welsh brothers. The other effect was to lower safety standards, increase the injury rate and induce men to take greater and greater risks to secure more money. This was something the NUM had fought since the days of the owners and had hoped would never be reintroduced in the nationalised industry, they were wrong. Its impact slowed and started to reverse the long trend of better and better safety scores. "In the years 1980 to 1988 the number of pits and employment fell by over half, but while the numbers of deaths in proportion likewise fell, the number of serious and major accidents did not. Extracts from annual reports of Mines Inspectorate show :

1980 "The number of reportable accidents in coal mines in 1980 increased by 6.7% compared with 1979 from 473 to 512."
1983 "In recent years there has been an increase in accidents, a trend which must be carefully watched."
1986/87: "The effect of the new arrangements for reporting accidents was to increase the number classified in the year as "major injuries" by about 30%. The increase in accidents compared with the previous year is 34.4 % but as there are fewer employees the trend is not satisfactory."[47]

"Not only has the major injury rate increased following the introduction of the incentive scheme in 1978 but since 1979 the incidence of underground fires has doubled. Just as worrying have been the attempts to water down the Mines and Quarries Act 1954."
Peter Heathfield and Peter McNestry
Gen. Secs of NUM and NACODS Joint Statement March 1989.

Latest figures as revealed in Labour Research Dec. 95 covering the first year of privatisation show a 28% increase in serious accidents and a rising death toll, "the Mines Inspectorate has collated an overall figure for major accidents nationally, the private coal companies have proved reluctant to provide detailed figures for their own pits to the unions as British Coal used to do." In fact our direct experience shows that the figures such as they are record only

47) LRD & H&SE Op Cit.

a small percentage of even serious accidents and virtually non of the minor ones.

It should be noted that prior to the sell off of British Coal all the respective private mine owners bidding for the pits made it clear to the government that they would not take them on unless the extensive safety legislation built up over decades were massively cut back.

Large areas of safety legislation have now been removed along with the role of the mine Deputy whose chief role was safety implementation, and a great relaxation on the stringent roof control regulations. The other factor weakening the safety trend in fact halting the declining injury rate was the introduction of private mine firms, 'contractors'. The figures for these were quoted earlier, now that the whole industry is privatised we have already started to see the process fall into steep degeneration, despite our efforts as a Union to stop the rot. In Summary the overall picture of the nationalised industry, by far safer than the private owners, but not *safe* as such, a <u>feature</u> of the class war which is perpetually fought over whoever sits in the management office, or on the government benches in Parliament.

"What have the glorious Miners Union done to prevent the shedding of more than a million jobs in this industry alone?"

We are asked. The mass closures started in the mid-1920's with the opening up of the Indian coal industry and the Ruhr coming into full production. The coal owners demanded in response more hours and less wages to stay in business. The reply of the miners and the MFGB in the words of Arthur Cook our president was "Not a penny off the pay, not a minute on the day!". We struck! We went to the TUC for support and a general strike was declared, millions of workers came out. The government declared a state of emergency, put the army on the streets, called up a volunteer force of middle class scabs, jailed progressive MPs, arrested the entire Executive Committee of the CPGB and rounded up other dissidents for detention. Baldwin the Prime Minister told the TUC General Council that they had better prepare their revolutionary government, since this was a challenge to the very constitution, they in turn shit themselves and stabbed the miners in the back. Calling off the general strike nine days after it began, although millions upon millions of workers defied the order or came out for the first time. The 'leadership' of the left split between those who fell in behind the TUC General Council and 'The Official Movement' and those who thought a left base built behind the miners action would pose an anti capitalist alternative to the TUC. Trotsky had taken something of this opinion, while Joe thought "the discipline of the class" had to be maintained behind the TUC. The Communist Party's position was to subordinate itself to the "labour lefts" following the line of the Communist International dominated at that time by Stalin and Bukharin. In May 1925 the *Anglo-Russian Committee* was composed jointly of Russian trade unions and The British TUC ostensibly to forge international trade union solidarity to stop imperialist intervention.

Stalin regarded a bloc with the TUC essential for the "defence" of the USSR.[48]

They maintained their presence on this committee during and after the betrayal of the British miners, thus lending a "left face" to the scoundrels of the General Council. After all the CPGB had already given over all political authority to the misleaders with their slogan *"All Power To The TUC General Council"*. Having thus conceded *"All Power"* to the class traitors one could hardly be too surprised when they stamped on you with it. The miners, my Da and Grandparents included, were left to fight on alone, in their case for a further nine months. My Granda was laid up ill from the effects of noxious fumes and dust in the mines, whilst me Da was 14 and had to try and scrounge what he could, barely living from soup kitchens, and weeds, they nearly starved to death. On the streets the tanks escorted middle class blacklegs to docks and staiths, while me Da along with others were dispersed from demonstrations by armed marines with fixed bayonets clearing the streets. War ships sailed up the Tyne and Clyde and mounted police with sabres rode through the villages dispersing pickets and their supporters. Scab trams, buses and trains were attacked, and the miners and their families fought back with everything they had, stones, sabotage clubs and barricades and sheer determination to win, but we lost. With the defeat came an onslaught on jobs and conditions which raged for a full decade following the collapse of the strike, the Union and the miners themselves barely survived.

Into this period came the rise of fascism. Hundreds of miners from the villages of Northumberland, Durham and Scotland and the valleys of Wales went off to Spain, in an act of selfless internationalist solidarity to fight against Franco and the fascists. In the run up to World War Two the government more and more intervened into the mines to ensure enough war production, this involved ever increasing amounts of capital investment, machines to displace pure muscle power and increase production for their war effort. Emergency Powers were introduced to stop miners and other key workers going on strike and damaging war production. Despite this, and victimisation, jailings and fines we continued to strike in greater and greater numbers as the war progressed. It should be said that the activities of Union leaders, some from the MFGB with 'red' reputations included, in an effort to save "the workers' state" (The USSR) were prepared to vigorously try and suppress our efforts to defend our own terms and conditions here.[49] The period after the war was one of euphoria and great expectations particularly among NUM leaders over nationalisation. The defeat of fascism, the first thrill of a Labour Government elected by a landslide poll of millions of people, many of them still

---

48) We seen something of a re-run of this duplicity in the 84/85 miners strike when premier Gorbachev met Thatcher and she had him promise her that the USSR would *not* support the British miners. Despite this 1M Roubles were raised by the Soviet miners in international solidarity, but because of the Soviet government pledge was never sent to the NUM as such, food aid was received but the British Customs refused to let it unload. Money was eventually received via the International Miners Organisation, the soviet money having been re-titled "for international purposes" (not specifically the NUM). The whole thing was used in a counter-revolutionary plot both here and in the USSR to discredit Arthur Scargill and international solidarity, by saying "the miners never received it, Arthur Scargill took it for himself." A scandalous lie, now thoroughly disproved. "Gorbachev was privately opposed to both the Soviet trade union coal and fuel embargo and to providing cash support, particularly once he had made a private commitment to Thatcher at their Chequers meeting in Dec. 1984. The Kremlin dispute was an early taste of emerging divisions at the heart of the Soviet Communist Party." — The Enemy Within, Seamus Milne.
49) See, Coal Communities In Conflict, for a record of mining militancy during the war years.

armed, demanding a clean sweep of the old injustices. The coal industry "ours" new conciliation arrangements, and national agreements took the union out of immediate conflict with
the government as such, although at branch and sometimes Area level, strikes still raged,
ancient battles over job control and rejection of supervision continued. Victor Allen describes it thus:-

"What did collaboration involve? It wasn't simply a case of co-operation with the NCB in
evolving policies for the coal industry but of accepting NCB. polices as its own and being in
part responsible for their application and execution. It meant moderating union demands,
sometimes almost to the point of extinction, at a time when the union was in a powerful market
position..it took action against miners who engaged in unofficial strikes and absenteeism. It
accepted pit closures and diffused local strikes about them. Collaboration didn't stop with
the demise of the Labour Government in 1951, not when the experiences of nationalisation
started to turn sour after 1956, when the decline of the industry first started the officials of the
union tended to blame it upon Conservative policy decisions but fairly quickly they came to
accept the logic of the case for contracting the industry. The political divisions amongst the
miners reflected differences in emphasis not basic attitudes. Communist Party members such
as Will Paynter the General Secretary from 1959, Bill Whitehead, who succeeded Paynter as
the President of the South Wales miners, Abe Moffat the President of the Scottish miners and
his brother Alex who succeeded him as well as others in official positions around the coalfields
continued to advocate continuity in the unions policy of co-operation with the NCB. They
were in agreement on this issue with those who were their political antagonists, such as
Sidney Ford, the union president, Sam Bullough the president of the Yorkshire Area and Jack
Lalley President of the Midland Area...On the question of contraction it insisted that the
decisions to close which pits when and where, were the prerogative of the management. The
union intervened only to facilitate the closures by assisting to alleviate the hardships which
might result from them. From the beginning of the contraction until 1964 when the Conservative
Government was still in office, the union officials constantly repeated that the only guarantee
of stopping the decline was to return a Labour government. Abe Moffat the President of the
Scottish Area stated in 1961 that "if we are going to solve our problems in the mining industry,
the best guarantee is to get this Tory government out of office." A Labour government was
returned in 1964. A year later it published its National Plan which indicated that it accepted
the reasoning of the previous Conservative government about energy resources and intended,
therefore to continue the contraction programme. The rate of closures was in fact intensified."[50]

It was against this scandalous and treacherous history of the unions misleaders at national
and most area levels that the unofficial movement of 1969 drawn from a diversity of groups
and rank and file bodies found its feet and declared war on the people who had effectively
taken the union from us and used its authority against us.[51] That movement aimed at remov-
ing the obstructions, the leaders, officials, constitutions, and demoralisation. To do it we had
to confront the entrenched 'old left' the Communist Party, among others, to which many of

---

50) The Militancy Of The British Miners, V.L.Allen, Moor Press Shipley, 1981.
51) A parallel struggle was taken place at the same in time our sister organisation in the United States,
although in conditions very much more severe with Unofficial leaders being shot and their families bombed
and activists killed and beaten. Our *Mineworker* and their *Miners Voice* kept in close liaison.

these class traitors belonged to (Theo will not accept any of this, since according to him 1969, and the Unofficial Movement just didn't happen). Through the 1980s the union prepared for action with many a false start and deliberate derailment too, against the impending new closure plans. Forcing a back down in 1981, then launching an overtime ban in 1983 and finally breaking into all out strike in 1984/85. During this time it was my turn to go through what my Da and Granda had done some 58 years previously, against the same Tory scum and stitched up by the same TUC's refusal to fight and 'Labour' leadership singing the praises of the class enemy. In 1984-85, I and my family along with hundreds of thousands of others threw everything flesh and blood could throw into the struggle against closures (since Theo thinks NUM officials aren't the same as other workers I wont bore him with the hardships we faced).

What did we do to stop job losses?

If you mean the back stabbing leaders of the post war years right up until the 60s, they did bugger-all, in fact wrong, they assisted the process. We do not class these characters as 'The Union' they are not worthy of the name, they are better described as *class collaborationist bosses men*, who betrayed the trust of tens of thousands of miners and misused the authority of the NUM to help weaken the union almost to the point of death. WE however, fought, with petrol bombs, with sabotage, with strikes, with iron railings, with motorway blockades, with train derailments, with clubs, in pitched battle's with police and the full paraphernalia of the state, we were starved, beaten, jailed, seriously injured and killed, in both the epoch struggles of 1926 and 1984. WE fought ; now let me ask you one Theo, what use were YOU or any of your critic colleagues, in such struggles of the working class, then or now?

What was YOUR contribution to these epoch events, because I seem to have missed it. What did you DO or have you ever done, to further the interests of working people and the fight for the working class? The answer is *NOWT!* Your 'do nothing but stand back and criticise' attitude, may not be as bad as those bastards from within our own ranks who turned the blades in our backs, but don't pretend you've found some shiny pure revolutionary alternative to slugging it out against coal bosses and when necessary union bosses,within the collective organisations of the miners, the NUM, because you haven't. Your alternative is ... nothing!

One vaguely gets the glimmer of an impression from Theo's writing that seems to suggest he thinks if the mines hadn't have been nationalised this mass closure programme wouldn't have taken place. Perhaps *couldn't* have taken place, because the NUM, would have fought the owners but didn't fight the NCB (at least in the post war years up to the 1960s). This is doubtful, in any case the war torn coalition government virtually took over the mines in those years because the owners were too inefficient, and basically *tight* to run them sufficiently well enough to get coal out in the required quantities to fuel the war. If the end of the war had not produced a labour government pledged to nationalisation it presumably would either a) Had a post war revolutionary situation developing far to left of any left sounding Labour alternative, with millions boycotting the election and using their contraband world war two arms toward a revolution, which if successful would mean you are right or b) Elected Church-ill the hater of things Union and left, in which case you are wrong because the process would have accelerated off the scale with all stops being pulled out for the development of nuclear energy, (which labour only tinkered with). It is also possible of course that had that happened the viciously "anti-red" Churchill who had earlier dreamed of the Nazi's wiping the Russians out, would have enthusiastically fallen in with covert US plans to drop an A-bomb on the USSR, and brought about World War Three. Whichever, I can see no yellow brick road down which the miners and the class would have gone happily skipping were it not for Nationalisa-tion leading them astray. Once more one needs look at other European countries, your own for a start, to see the utter destruction of the post war coal industry *without* nationalisation.

Mechanisation is a welcome development in dangerous and physically exhausting manual coal face work, it reduces back breaking toil[52] in general it takes people further away from direct sources of danger such as the coal itself or the wall of the heading. In some cases it allowed for early retirement or redundancy for men over 50 on very reasonable terms. Had it been implemented as part of an overall package aimed at shortening the working week, bringing in earlier and earlier retirement without loss of wages this would have been ideal.

But you are right Theo the NUM did not manage to bring around a socialist revolution, and that is what it would take to bring around the things you think we should have done. What we did do was to resist all compulsory job losses and pit closures on three major occasions since the 1920s, we have launched mass campaigns to do it, but failed, not so much because the class enemy was stronger, but because *our side* the working class as a whole, and Trade Unionists in other industries didn't unite on our side as hard as the employers and their state did on theirs. That is a collective failure and cannot be laid at the door of the NUM and the miners.

As to the attempt to describe the industrially moderate political right wing of the NUM leadership in the 1930s through to the early '60s.I'm really quite well aware of it. I don't need to "listen to what some researchers from the University of Sussex found out about worker-union relations in the 1950s". I've written extensively on the subject myself. I KNOW there was a reactionary leadership in most of the coalfields until the movement of '69 (which Theo thinks didn't happen) dislodged them in what was a symptom of the growing militancy among the miners as a whole. Ignoring the views he quotes from, "the attitude of Ashton miners, and that of many others; the union is a prime necessity". Despite the leadership's accommodation of the bosses, he refuses to see not a leadership in conflict with the member-

---

52) My own class of work as a'stone worker' involved building 'a pack' a solid square of stone slabs on the outside, built dry stone wall fashion, up to the roof, and packed inside with smaller rocks, the total six yards long two yards wide, from floor to roof. It involved back breaking work, carrying huge slabs of rock bent double in cramped spaces, shovelling on your kneels, often up to your thighs in stinking water, in heat and dense dust for many hours. Two of us did that every day. In the early '90s this method was replaced by the erection of a thin wire cage which takes the place of the big slabs, into this is hung a large polythene bag. The bag is then fed from a hose pipe with premixed concrete. Instead of shovelling all day, you stick the hose pipe in the bag, and go and sit down for two hours. Exposure from roof falls is reduced from four or five hours to about ten minutes. There is no magic under capitalism of course, the system saved the broken back and bet knee but caused exposure to chemical burns and dermatitis. We welcome change to lessen toil and danger but not new dangers or the compulsory redundancies which eventually came in 1992-93.

ship over the political complexion and industrial orientation of the union, but an *anti-union* struggle between *the miners* and the NUM. The windingmen's strike you refer to was certainly sold out by the right wing Yorkshire area leadership of the period. BUT the windingmen were on strike in their NUM branch. This was a struggle **within the** union against the bureaucrats by a section of the membership. At times whole panels were in action together against official NUM policy and the Area &/or National leadership.

The whole movement against closures in 1980 and 1981 resulting in the quasi official national conference in London with president elect Arthur Scargill in support and the sitting president Joe Gormley firmly against and the NEC split down the middle were preludes to the divisions in 1984 between leaderships and areas *and members*. These are struggles *within* the NUM for control of the union and its direction. To try and present it as *the NUM* versus *The Miners* is just plain distortion. You cannot deliver an accurate analysis simply by inventing the situation such as you would like it to be, only as it actually is. As for "Union officials..in their soft dreams of harmonious union management relations" the last thirty years of bitter struggles in the coal industry would require that you were a sound sleeper indeed, and while some might have dwelt in such fanciful realms likewise many have not. The point is such dreamers even had they been common in the last thirty years do not characterise the struggles of the miners within the Union frequently against the leaderships through their Union.

The pages which Theo devotes to what he calls "shop stewards" seem to be a mysterious attempt to draft those traditions, particularly those from the massive car plants, into the pit environment. Presumably classing NUM Branch Committee persons or Branch Officials as "shop stewards". "It is really amazing how Douglass manages to write so enthusiastically about the unofficial movement i.e. the shop stewards (the left?) taking over in the union to force it on the course of official strikes in 1972 and 1974, and at the same time to remain dead silent about the transformation of the role of the shop stewards at plant level, turning them into a major element of a policy of establishing a new plant consciousness (and thus ruining whatever might have been left of the radical image). It is reassuring no doubt, to see that this policy failed as well, in spite of all the unswerving dedication of shop stewards and convenors in making it work. The normalisation of procedures and the rise of consultation/participation (linked to the more widespread use of the check-off system) has been of overriding importance in this respect. Procedural machinery itself contained a higher element of common interest. If the parties were aware that they must make the rules to regulate conditions of work they were not only committed to machinery for making these rules but also to machinery for applying and interpreting them. They were also committed to some means of dealing with grievances, whether these were likely to be formulated into collective agreements of a formal kind or not. This was finally bound to increase the area of joint consultation in which management took union officials and shop stewards more into their confidence in order to broaden the basis of understanding between the parties.

Expressed in very general terms, procedures were both treaties of peace and devices for avoidance of war between shop stewards/ union officials and management's as a specialist in industrial relations studies so nicely put it."[53]

---

53) Theo Sanders, Op Cit. pp42-43.

Of course we can see what your talking about, and the scene is quite familiar, however its not *necessarily* like that, it depends upon the complexion of the particular body its 'culture' political outlook, and motive, the type of workplace being operated in, management's attitudes to unions and workers having any say at all. It depends on the outside political climate, and the prevalent attitude of the working class in general, or in that region and plant in particular. It is entirely circumstantial and contextual, it is not a blue print or train line down which all unions follow or workplace representative necessarily conform to.

In our case (and we are discussing the NUM) it is just not applicable, at least in the last decade or so of so called industrial relations at pit level. At Hatfield industrial relations would not be put so nicely, with an activist pushing his cigarette into the face of an undermanager at a 'consultation' meeting, or another Undermanager attacking me with a pick at a 'conciliation' meeting, or a branch committee man and Undermanager squaring up in the pit yard. The Manager and the Union secretary frequently had to be dragged from each others throats, while court injunctions were served against us by Coal Board lackeys protected by police vans. The air was anything but harmonious, cups of tea stopped being supplied at meetings because they often got flung around the room, as did telephones. Finally Union officials were not invited to meetings, consultation was abolished, all contracts had to be imposed, time off for union duties was punishable with the sack, officials were given the most isolated or dangerous jobs at the pit, on the worst shift patterns as the union at branch level was totally derecognised, as it had been at national level for the preceding 11 years. Perhaps the scene in the 1950's MAY have been more like the one you describe, though judging from the stormy industrial relations of the period it clearly does not characterise the NUM *member* or the NUM meeting, which contrary to your view have *always* even to the last been *mass* assemblies of very vociferous workers. Nobody I have shown your work to, would recognise <u>any</u> of what one supposes are meant to be pit branch scenarios. They are however very similar to those conjured up by the British tabloid press, the all powerful shop convenor, a law unto himself, contemptuous of workers and management alike, hand in the till, etc.[54]

Miners union branches just will not match up to such an image, though members might have many complaints, of lack of combativity, remoteness from specific jobs or groups etc. still others will complain of too much militancy, too much politics. **Did anyone ever say the NUM Branch was some organisational immaculate conception?** Nothing that I have written, spoken or experienced has ever given that view, the NUM is a microcosm of the class war, conflictual, conciliatory, contradictory, and always in a state of political and industrial character fluctuation. It has been central in the life struggles of tens of thousands of miners and their families, it is not some final solution to class organisation, it was framed in the fire of conflict and bears many birth marks from capitalism and backward social attitudes picked up from capitalist society at large, but it has been by and large an instrument of class struggle in the cause of the pit communities, it is certainly ***not*** the alien outside enemy force described by Theo and his comrades.

---

54) Indeed there are great similarities between Theo's picture of industrial relations and the reactionary British film comedy of the 1950's "I'm All Right Jack".

CAJO BRENDEL

MY REPLY, TO HIS REPLY, TO MY REPLY, TO HIM !!

In Cajo and his comrades we see the classical embodiment of petit-bourgeois idealism, first come the pre-conceived set of conclusions and then the facts are either selected or adapted to fit them. So we set off from the conviction that "Unions", per se, are counter- revolutionary, pro establishment instruments of the state developed to oppress working people and keep them under the yoke of capitalism.

At the same time it cannot be said that workers don't fight back, not least at work. How can we make the former fact match the earlier conclusion? A quick sleight of the wrist shows Unions, hold back, stamp on and support the bosses, while all struggles at work, regardless of the organisations (i.e. Trade Unions) they take place in, are 'autonomous' "outside and against" trade unions. It matters not that the struggle takes place 99 times out of 100 *in or through* Unions or that militants cited in the struggle may themselves be stewards, officials or anyway activists closely associated *with* the union, ipso-facto if its a struggle its *anti* the union, if it's anything derogatory it is an example *of* the union. It follows from this that all Officials of the Unions from top to bottom are reactionary, self serving bosses' men, by definition, and our backside foremost "analysis" they *must* be. So it is that the "Answer" asserts that the pitmen in 1972 ran the strike activity "themselves", not "The NUM". When actually they were *the same people.*

"... it could be described as a general strike organised from the bottom, a sort of general wildcat which started not because of the will and authority of a Union, imposing its tactics on the workers, but because of the workers activity by themselves and for themselves and thus imposing their will on the Union."[55]

Well O.K. I would argue that that's what happened in '72-74, '84-85 and a thousand strikes in-between, but it also happened to be *following* a national conference of the Union decided on a specific wage demand, and after the successful conduct of a national ballot, *all of which* was administered through the union. How does this differ from "The Miners" in 1926? Contrasting 1926 to the post war period, Cajo observes:-

"... they (The Unions) could no longer allow themselves the luxury of a big strike, not even one limited to a particular area or trade. This fact has ever since been a decisive factor in the behaviour of workers ..."[56]

Which would be extraordinary if true, the largest strikes ever have taken place *post* war,

55) Answer To David Douglass, Cajo Brendel, Goodbye to Unions Op Cit.
56) Ibid.

including those of steelworkers, mineworkers, railworkers, printers and others. If this factor "forms the subject of a large part of the book" i.e. his book, it is fatally flawed by events of those decades, which confront his thesis head on.

For a man presumably (this is another guess) in the Anarchist camp, Cajo has some touchingly *Leninist* concepts of workers "false-consciousness". After conceding that many workers wouldn't take the betrayal of individual leaders as a sign that "the Unions" were *against* the workers he rationalises:-
"If they often were not yet aware that what they were doing was in total contradiction with union practice and party principles, their struggles effectively created this contradiction and intensified it more and more."

The reality comrade, is that workers were *entirely conscious* of the contradictory elements within the union apparatus and have *consistently* used its class struggle component to *confront* the bureaucracy, the boss and at times the Tory or Labour government. None of this makes workers "anti-Union" these are consciously Trade Unionists and revolutionary workers in unions engaging in struggle for justice and bread. They understand the limitations of the Trade Union apparatus *because they more often than not confront it.*

We however do not conclude from this that "unions" are anti working class or that class actions are "anti the unions". None of the examples you site, remotely fit the proposition.

My perception of Unions, workers in Unions, Conflicts in and within Unions are as developed in this pamphlet, it is diametrically opposed to the mechanical and non-scientific approach adopted by Cajo. It is also a fact as a life long revolutionary worker, and at times miners union official I refuse to be libelled as "in the enemy camp" by some petit- bourgeois tortuous thinking.

Cajo's "Answer" in Goodbye To The Unions offers little new. I concede to not having known the document I read was not an original of his, or that it had been gutted in parts and adaptations made entirely without his approval or even his knowledge. Necessarily parts of my response, especially to these pieces are flawed, in so far as HE didn't write them. I pick him up on a number of factual points, which turn out to be not his, and were correct in the original work. Likewise I concede that my description of his views as "situationist" were incorrect for the reasons described in this pamphlet, I hadn't heard of Council Communists, and thought the views I was reading looked like those of the situationists I had encountered in the early 1970s. Cajo is also correct in pointing out my mistaken citing of the struggle in the so called "Winter of Discontent" as 1975 instead of 1978, this was due to reliance on memory rather than checking the date.

That said, and having now had the chance of reading the original and complete script for which I thank Cajo, the main antipathy of our two view points remain fundamental differences of class perception, & analysis of class struggle in the world of work and industry.

Apart from these main planks of difference there are a host of minor conflicts of fact and perception. The comments on 1926 are ill informed, more workers struck *after* TUC called off the strike than before, and makes a lie to the tale that it was a bureaucratic led strike "with no popular support".

The proposition that nationalisation of the coal industry was "simply no difference between private and nationalised capitalism" has been thoroughly shot to death in the last chapter responding to Sanders. Sufficient to say we are now in the post nationalisation period and we as miners can already see the massive adverse differences despite our bitter years of struggle against the nationalised bosses.

Cajo suggests "In Place Of Strife" was supported by "The Unions" as part of "The Unions" attempt to suppress wildcats. In fact In Place Of Strife was *bitterly* opposed by the trade unions as a whole and universally ignored. But in this case, as with the other slights of hand, he asserts (my emphasis), "The Unions ... had no intention (and no means) of fighting the law seriously. The Workers however did fight it ..." He then goes on to quote the host of Trade Union battles of the period, the postal workers strike, the UCS Joint Shop Stewards Committee "work in". These are cited as examples of "The Workers" fighting, whereas "The Unions" did not. "The hardest blow against it (The Industrial relations Act '72) came from three major conflicts during the first seven months of the year. Strikes of the miners, the railwaymen and the dockers." Don't be coy, Cajo, that's the NUM, the NUR / ASLEF and the TGWU — *ALL OF THEM TRADE UNIONS.* It is not only handy but necessary if you claim Cajo's perception to be able to cite 'Workers' in struggle *despite* their membership of, and clear support for, their unions. If you could not, think of the conclusions to be drawn from his observation that the strikes "escalated to the point of a catastrophic showdown ... directly between the working class and the state." They did indeed, but this class was organised in UNIONS. This fact proves impossible to bend into the theory no matter how hard you try:-
"What formally looked like official action in essence was not." "In essence?" meaning, it's the kind of UNION action that contradicts the kind you prefer to cite which suit your preconceived conclusion? It doesn't fit, so therefore this isn't 'normal' union activity. The whole point **is** however that union responses *differ* and can be militant, moderate, bureaucratic, wildcat of any combination or station in between.

The central plank upon which the whole edifice of council communism stands, is that the working class has been held back from achieving its liberation *by the existence of trade unions.* That had trade unions NOT existed the working class would be that much less constrained, more combative, and less prone to derailment.

It is a fanciful conclusion, not least because "the working class" is not *born* into the world with a conscious understanding of its own exploitation, let alone a universal conclusion that the active overthrow of capitalism and all exploiting hierarchies is the sole solution and task of life. Volumes could be filled demonstrating this most obvious point alone. All revolutionary struggles and change has been directed not only at the exploiting class but also the ideology of and acceptance of such by the exploited. The class struggle is a struggle in the main to build class consciousness to form an ideology of resistance in contrast to the ideology of acceptance. As demonstrated throughout this work, this is a struggle that takes place

WITHIN the union daily. The struggle to establish unions at the moment is not frequently beset by heroic arguments from the class that they want MORE struggle than that on offer from the unions. But on the contrary are fearful about defeat, unemployment and lack class confidence. Forming a union is often a **bold** step for most workers, which poses the question of class struggle *DIRECTLY*, in their own lives in a way which it did not do so before. When the reformed IWW in Britain began recruiting in the void left by non unionism per se, it did *not* encounter factories and services full of people who were MORE combative MORE revolutionary and class conscious by virtue of their non unionism. They found people yet to be convinced of the *possibility* of combined, collective class action for the here and now, improvement of living and working conditions as well as more far reaching conclusions on the possibility of all out revolutionary class war. In countries and places we encounter non unionism in, either because they have been ruthlessly crushed and wiped out by employers or else have not been allowed to develop, why do we not see the inextinguishable flames of conflict which have not had the unions smothering them? Why are we not witnessing unrestrained class struggle without the fetters of bureaucrats and parasites and unions? Why on the contrary are the places where unions are not in existence on a national or world scale generally the MOST exploited and impoverished? I suggest, because the lack of unions is the result of the lack of class strength and consciousness and strong employers and states which have determined to prevent the union developing is in order to keep the worker in a state of super-exploitation. If as you say, the unions do such a good job for the employers why is union organisation in most parts of the world repressed, by sacking, the blacklist, imprisonment, torture and murder? Such is the history of class organisations in places like Latin America, Asia, and Indo-china. Whilst the United States itself has virtually eradicated the unions by the most ruthless and often murderous campaign.

Individual union leaders and union structures have in *many* places, where the challenge was strong from the class, attempted to derail and hold back the movement. True. The non existence of Unions does NOT however mean that that challenge would have taken place in the first place, let alone that it would have gone onto complete victory. These are crude simplistic notions which the modern industrial history of the world dispute at every turn.

The conclusion drawn from the Webbs, that there was more labour unrest in Britain before the organisation of 'Unions' than after is mistaken on at least two counts. The Webbs huge pioneering work on Unions is flawed like many other subsequent observers by their petit-bourgeois preconception of what they were observing. Because they came from the world of learning and literature, of written records, of accounts and consistency, they judged the development of workers organisations by how far they conformed to such middle class precepts of organisation. With the top hatted artisans and craftsmen, the educated aristocrats of labour they found kindred souls developing Trade Unions on models of the craft guilds, with formal ceremonies, minutes, written records, statements of accounts and educated speech. The unskilled, untutored, illiterate labourer on the other hand had to wait until ideologically motivated artisans and craftsmen carried the message and model of trade Unionism down to the labouring classes in the 1890s "New Unionism". It was a canny tale but utterly untrue! Thousands perhaps millions of labour history students have been misled into following the trail of the totally mythical creature "new unionism". In the process they ignore and are taught not to see decades and centuries of unionism among Seamen, Dockers, Miners and labourers of all sorts who had existed, fought won and lost monumental battles without the needs of minutes, bank accounts, fixed organisation or continuity for hundreds of years BEFORE the so called "New Unions" emerged. That the Webbs knew of their existence is without doubt, but they ignored them partly because of class bias and basic ignorance and partially because they didn't last. They weren't preserved with organisation hierarchies and records but instead were laid down or disassembled at the end of each epoch of struggle, only to be reconstituted anew when needed at some point in the future. To the Webbs however a trade union BY DEFINITION must be " a continuous association of wage labourers" if it isn't continuous, it isn't a union. Therefore when they record struggles "before" union organisation, they are actually talking OF union organisation in reality, baring titles such as "combinations" "associations" "bonds" or "brotherhoods" they were combinations of workers coming together to fight against work and wage exploitation = unions, whether the Webbs criteria fitted them or not.

The second reason is that labour unrest is cyclical, it has rises and falls quite independent of the strength of unions in numbers or density terms. It is related to a host of other factors, bargaining power, general social political conditions prevailing outside the workplace, the level of perceived consciousness and combativity, take the current tide of national general strikes in France organised around a minute Trade Union Movement. Even if we accepted the Webbs eccentric definition of unions, it is perfectly possible that labour unrest would fall for a period coinciding with union 'organisation' but that would not be _due_ to that fact, and would soon rise again (as in fact it did) regardless of the numerical existence of unions. The rise in general class consciousness and revolutionism in May '68 France took millions of unorganised workers onto the streets on strike alongside the minority organised workers. This was not because they were unorganised or organised but despite the fact in that period.

When Cajo turns specifically to look at periods in the miners history rather like the Webbs themselves he is unable to understand what he sees. Of course the checkwieghman paid for by the men to keep the tonnage records and therefore their wages legally correct and prevent robbery by the employers, was sometimes the target of blackmail and bribery by the employers. It is also true that any such trusted person misusing the collective trust of the miners would a) Soon be sacked by them (This is why the miners refused to allow the employers to pay his wages) and b) Would go literally in fear of his life throughout the entire country. Class vengeance was rather swift and nasty in the C19th, as even bourgeois historians will attest to. A similar regime was attendant upon our workers safety inspectors. having won by industrial action and moral outrage at the carnage and destruction on the C19th mines, the right to appoint and pay our own safety inspectors, free from the control of the owners and later the nationalised bosses, great prestige and trust fell upon such men.

Some may indeed have been seduced by the offer of a quiet life in a hard world to turn a blind eye to safety impediments and potential disaster; the men however would not be long in picking up the discrepancy especially if accidents followed favourable s.123 inspector reports. "A bosses' man" in a position of workmen's inspector or checkweighman was, however, a virtual contradiction in terms. The men were after all chosen from the miners' own ranks, paid by the miners directly, lived cheek by jowl with their fellows and subject to immediate dismissal, infringements of class trust carry severe censor, especially in the violent and volatile pit community of the C19th. The offer of a nice 8am shift in exchange for NOT reporting a hazard or faulty scales might seem attractive to those looking in, but those who understand the dire wrath of a closed community and its unremitting vengeance will know that only an unprincipled and damn foolhardy person would ignore the consequences of class collaboration and betrayal. But it happened at times, as it did when previously folk of upstanding scabbed or the local Club committee person was found with their fingers in the bar till / the benevolent fund / old folks treat money. But this periodical seduction by capitalist mores does not however render null and void the overall endeavour, or the principle and goal to which it is directed, that being to assist one's fellow workers.

Cajo's position would be a little stronger if he once conceded at any point in history, not what we at times have *failed* to achieve, but what and why we strove to achieve it in the first place. Unions were not, are not instruments 'invented' to hold down the class but its opposite, despite having developed organisational dysfunctional roles at top level, and self serving hierarchies which conflict with the central purpose for the union's existence, which is defence and progress of the class.

"The struggle for the eight hour day may have been led by engineers in the 1890s, <u>but certainly not by the district unions in the British coal industry. To tell the simple truth, such apostles of trade unionism among miners like Burt in Northumberland and Crawford in Durham were so busy getting their unions confirmed by employers and to enter into amicable relations of conciliation and arbitration with them that they clearly opposed any proposals for a legally enacted eight- hour day for hewers (guess why just the hewers!)</u>"[57]

Well the bare facts are nearly right, The Northumberland and Durham miners DID oppose the effort to get the hewers onto an 8 hour day, indeed they left the Miners Federation and disaffiliated over the issue. Burt and Crawford were *strictly instructed by the miners* not to accept it, although they vacillated and wormed to try and get out of the opposition, the owners thought the 8 hour day was the best thing since slavery, because my dear old comrade to tell the simple truth :-

The hewers of Durham and Northumberland already worked a maximum seven hour and more usually six hour day! and while they would have accepted a reduction for the boys and outbye men to 8 hours these were still to carry on working up to 12 hours in the northern coalfields and even more elsewhere.

In addition the hewers had always worked two overlapping shifts, commonly six hours each, the eight hour day was to introduce three shifts including for the first time blasting and hewing coal on a night shift, the only time when traditionally the mine was allowed to clear of dust, and gas and be ventilated. The question was inextricably linked to the policy of restriction of output. In a depressed coal market, production on three rather than two shift cycles

---

57) Answer, Cajo Brendel, Op Cit. p31 (my emphasis).

meant a massive increase in production, a fall in the selling price, and since wages were linked to the vend (the sale price of coal) the eight hour day was a direct reduction in wages.

For thirty years the eight hour day had been fought in the northern coalfields, when in 1910 it was finally introduced after an agreement between the leaders of the DMA without the knowledge let alone consent of the men, hell broke out. On Dec. 24 1909 the terms of the agreement were released in the local newspapers under the heading "Eight Hours Act: Agreement between owners and miners". When the agreement was introduced on January 1st 1910 widespread strikes, mass meetings of lodges, protest marches and riot broke out all over the county.

At the beginning of the third week of January a few of the striking lodges had gone back to work but feeling elsewhere was running high. On Monday Jan 17th an army of miners 10,000 strong invaded Gateshead to demonstrate against John Johnson a DMA official who was standing for election. The men arrived at mid-day headed by three brass bands. They carried banners one of which read "We are the South Moor Miners! Down with Johnson, the three shift candidate, the miners ruination!" To make the point on their way home they attacked the pit at Birtley where work had recommenced. The authorities had been warned and barricaded the gates.

"The railing were speedily demolished, and a rush was made for the pit, but there was a surprise in store for the miners, as they were met by a force of police and men in the employment of the Birtley iron Company, numbering about 100. The defenders were all armed with heavy walking sticks, and many of the miners carried pieces of broken railings and stones. Several scrimmages took place, and then the police laid about them vigorously. There was a strong reply, and two of the policemen several of the miners were somewhat injured about the head by blows from sticks and stones. Another force of police appeared in the rear, and they eventually succeeded in driving off the invaders and preventing them reaching the pit."[58]

If this was the conclusion of the march it had started out no less lively. Marley Hill colliery was raided by young miners. Between 4,000 and 5,000 miners had left the Stanley district to join the Gateshead demonstration. As they passed the pit, about 400 "young'uns" broke away and charged the colliery. They turned over tubs, smashed windows and looted the offices. They hurled debris down the shaft and armed themselves with pick shafts with which they demolished the lamp cabin and tool store.[59]

This is not the place to tell the whole story of the violent resistance to the hated 8 hour system (the owners compromised and made it 7 but retained the night shift which was an

---

58) The Durham Chronicle, 14 Jan 1910.
59) A full discussion of this and the battles over restriction of output takes place in my early work Pit Life In Co. Durham, pub History Workshop, Oxford. Sharp eyed readers will detect from this work that 23 years ago I too talked about "The Union" in opposition to the "The Miners", and meant by this the leaders of the Union. Although it is patently clear from the text which is full of local union branch resistance and unofficial union activity, and radical union leaders that I am not attacking unions as such. Such an interpretation would never had occurred to me at the time, had it done so I would have been more specific.

even greater burden) suffice it say, opposition to it was far from the foolish and reactionary act of betrayal but quite its opposite.

It is likewise not necessary to trade blow for blow with Cajo on historic events in our mining history, he presents as is his thesis, right wing stalwarts of moderation and reaction like Burt, Crawford and Wilson as The Miners Union, ignoring the violent, vociferous and widespread militant and at times revolutionary opposition of the miners branches and local leaders. He recommends that people who wish to know what was going on should read these traitors versions of our history as well as that of Welbourne the Master of Cambridge College, a man whose class bias and contempt for militant unionism among the miners is clear. Wilson, whose leadership of the DMA. is legendary in its conservatism and collaboration and who had concluded there was no longer any class war or point in conflict between owners and miners, is presented as the voice of the *UNION*. But comrade, when Follonsby Lodge secretary, Area Executive member and Industrial Unionist *George Harvey* wrote his "Does John Wilson Serve The Interests Of The Working Class" a work that caused him to be brought to court by the infamous leader for libel, whose voice was that? Harvey had penned the article loudly proclaiming Wilson to be an enemy of the working class and a servant of capitalism, a charge he repeated in the court citing as example Wilson's agreement to a 5% reduction in wages which even a bourgeois umpire had held to be unwarranted, whose voice was this? Wasn't this too, in reality ANOTHER countervailing voice of the miners union? I suggest it was.

Likewise Cajo takes as gospel the Webbs' definition of the militant and radical times "before the forming of unions" since miners' unions outwith this definition were around from some time in the 1700s and were highly combative to say the least, when exactly was this time "before the forming of Unions"? We have mined coal in Tyneside since 1100 on a commercial footing and always been rebellious but whether we were more so in the years before our early unions I very much doubt. I doubt that this would be true even under a strict utility of the Webbs' limited definition.

Overall Conclusion

How we address the class struggle is not ultimately determined by the immense material we have in our heads, nor can we construct from our book of favourite things the composition of the working class such as we would like to see it, we cannot reinvent the working class to look more like a 1930s Spanish CNT because we are Anarchists, or to look more like the Petrograd Soviet because we are Leninists. We must address the class such as it is composed NOW, in its organisational class forms such as they actually are. We cannot abstain from British Trade Unions because they are not as sexy as Anarcho-Syndicalist continental or Scandinavian variations.

Because as this pamphlet has demonstrated the struggles of the class in the workplace DO take place, overwhelmingly IN trade unions, cutting ourselves off from this struggle or proclaiming WE Are Anti the Unions, is simply to cut oneself off from the working class. The traditions of Syndicalism such as they were are absorbed into the rail unions ASLEF and formally NUR (now RMT) while many see the slogan and tradition of ONE BIG UNION in the mass general, unionism of the TGWU and GMWU; whilst the nearest thing we have to a "red" industrial union is the NUM. The spirit of the IWW is carried into the rest of the labour movement by these living unions, not in prayers to the spirit of a stillborn CNT that never was. The class war is fought with the unions but also within the union, are we to join this fight, or abstain in some self serving act of political purity which actually hides a gross contempt for working people.

A lot of what is basically *CACA* for want of a better word, has been spoken and is being spoken about the "special nature of revolutionary organisation" let us be quite clear the ONLY thing an organisation requires in order that it be 'revolutionary' is a working class composition conscious of its own oppression, conscious of itself as a social class, and the determination to overthrow the existing order, to initiate a new form of society, based upon social, political and economic justice. To do this *__there is nothing to stop a trade union, a tenants association, or the regulars down the local boozer from constituting themselves as revolutionary organisation if they were all committed to that end.__* True the original design of the organisation may be ill fitted to its new role, but this is a minor detail which can be elaborated in struggle, The Revolution DOES NOT require some fundamental premise "The Existence of a Monolithically or Democratically, Centred Party Leninist" or otherwise; neither does it require some pristine and politically virginal/unsullied by trade union/social- democratic reformist, Anarchist Society or Federation. *It Requires only ... the revolutionary working class!*

Obviously those of us who have already been won to the ideology of revolutionary communism or anarchism, will wish to meet, plan, spread the word, research issues, issue educational documents etc. But the aim must be of infusing the working class *itself* in its daily struggles, with revolutionary ideology, not by ignoring such manifestations of class struggle as somehow inferior. Our aim should be *impel* the existing process of class war forward, not think somehow we have to re-invent it, making the unions function in a revolutionary manner, raising revolutionary ideas in the work place and within unions, never letting the bureaucracy dictate the terms or limit the imagination of workers in struggle. The formation of the IWW with activists from all over Britain can be greatly utilised in this process, with the formation of industrial and workplace cells, to act as revolutionary propagandists and activists within the workplace AND the Unions. The revolutionary anarchist and Marxist movement needs to keep its feet firmly in the base of mass class struggle, we should not be led off into the wide blue yonder of petulant petit-bourgeois idealism or the self imposed splendid isolation in our purer than thou abstentionism.

In the words of the song "It's not the fight you dreamed of, but the one you really fought!"

Let's engage the class struggle taking place before our eyes and re-raise the slogan of '68:

ALL POWER TO THE IMAGINATION!

Glossary

ANC. African National Congress, a broad based cross class democratic alliance, having within its ranks the mass of the militant black and revolutionary working class elements, at present.

BIFU. Bank Insurance and Finance Union.

Canny. Geordie usage, meaning in this context, cute.

CPGB. The Communist Party of Great Britain. In the context of this pamphlet this is the Provisional Central Committee of the CPGB who refused to fold up and die when the USSR collapsed and most Soviet based CPs shut up shop for the duration.

Caca. La'lands / Geordie dialect meaning SHIT, but of an endearing childish type.

PLO. The Palestine Liberation Organisation, major cross-class, multi factioned centre for Palestinian diplomatic, military and political affairs.

Zionist. Those Jews who believe that Jews are a nationality with a fixed country, and that country is Palestine, which they have renamed Israel, and to which the Jews of all countries of origin should emigrate to and support in the meantime. There are many Anti-Zionist Jews on both religious and political grounds, who think of Israel either as a blasphemy, or Racialist Ethnic imperialism.

Hezbolla. Muslim fundamentalists who desire a non secular Islamic regime and oppose both the Zionists and the Jews and all other non-believers as such.

Sinn Fein. In the context of this pamphlet, the Provisional Sinn Fein, political wing of the Provisional republican movement, which reformed following the abandonment of armed struggle by the Old IRA in the 70s and the emergence of Provisional IRA.

IRA. Irish Republican Army. In the context of this pamphlet the provisional IRA unless otherwise prefixed.

RMT. Rail Maritime and Transport Union

RCP. Revolutionary Communist Party.

ASLEF. Amalgamated Society Locomotive Enginemen and Firemen.

Rag-Up. The Miners, particularly those on the face work stripped to the skin, when a dispute breaks out the men dress again in their pit rags and walk out of the mine. It is largely a Yorkshire expression.

Panel. In the context of this pamphlet, the unofficial assemblies of Union branches based on coal board areas. Set up to check Executive powers, they became self acting semi-official regional Unions.

NEC. National Executive Committee.

Heading gate. The Tunnels into the coal faces.

IWW. The Industrial Workers Of the World. The world-wide revolutionary Industrial Union.

DMA. Durham Miners Association. The county union, which ultimately joined in with the National Union of Miners, which then affiliated to the Miners Federation of Great Britain, but then broke with that body for fifteen years over the 8 hours, three shift, question.

VEND. The saleable portion of mineral extracted from the mine, i.e. the saleable coal, or the price of that coal on the market.

Lodges. Branches of the miners union.

UDA. Ulster Defence Association, umbrella organisation for the Loyalist military.
UDM. Union Of Democratic Miners, the organisation of anti strike, blackleg miners.
EFA. European Fighter Aircraft of immense cost and uselessness.
NSM. National Socialist Movement, The British version of the German Nazi party ultimately led by Sir Oswald Mosley.
Gaffers. Assorted managers and bosses.
COSATU. Confederation of South African Trade Unions (the South African TUC).

BIBLIOGRAPHY

Goodbye To The Unions, Theo Sander & Cajo Brendel in Echanges Et Mouvement, Paris.
Organise, *organ of the ACF.*
Weekly Worker, *paper of the CPGB Provisional Central Committee.*
Analysis.
Subversion.
Autonomous Class Struggle In Britain 1945-1980, Cajo Brendel.
The Mineworker, Organ Of The Mineworkers Internationale, Doncaster.
Miners Voice, Organ of Miners For A Democratic Union, USA.
The Durham Chronicle.
The Guardian.
The Independent.
The Slaughter Of The Miners By the NCB, D Douglass, Socialist Union Press, Doncaster.
The Need For Workers Control In The Mining Industry, D Douglass, 1Vth International Publications, London.
Refracted Perspective, D Douglass.
Coal Communities In Conflict, D Douglass Special Edition Heavy Stuff, Class War.
Pit Sense Versus The State, D Douglass, Phoenix.
The Durham Miners, D Douglass, in Miners Quarrymen and Saltworkers, Ed Raph Samuel's, Routledge and Keegan Paul.
Pit Life In Co. Durham, D Douglass, History Workshop, Oxford.
A Miners Life, Douglass and Krieger, RKP.
The Heavy Stuff, *Class War Theoretical Periodical*
Outside And Against The Unions, Wildcat.
Anarchism And The Unions, Irish Workers Solidarity Movement, Dublin May 6th 92.
The Miners, Page Arnot.
The Miners Association, A Trade Union In The Age Of The Chartists, R Challiner.
The Enemy Within, Ian MacGreggor.
The Enemy Within, Seumas Milne.
The Militancy of the British Miners, Vic Allen. Moor Press, Shipley, 1981.
A History Of The Durham Miners Association, John Wilson. 1870-1904, Durham 1907.
Memories Of A labour Leader, John Wilson, London, 1910.
Does John Wilson MP Serve The Interests of The Working Class? George Harvey, in The Socialist. Edinburgh. 1910.
The Miners Unions Of Northumberland and Durham, Welbourne.

Manifesto Of The Socialist Union Internationalist, pt One 2nd edition Aug. 75.
The History Of Trade Unionism, Sidney and Beatrice Webb, 1890.
History Workshop Publications.
Masters and Servants, Huw Beynon and Terry Austrin, London 1994.
The Diary Of Bobby Sands, Sinn Fein Publicity Dept, Dublin 1981.
Spartacus, Organising Bulletin for Socialists in Norfolk and Suffolk, Oct. 94.
Syndicalism, Tom Brown.
Reports of HMI Mines and Quarries, HMSO.
Labour Research. LRD.
The Hazards Of Mining, LRD.

Appendix 1

Anti-Unionism Worldwide

Most of the anti union views expressed in this pamphlet are not only clearly anti working class they are peculiarly eurocentric at best and southerno-anglocentric at worse. In many third world countries workers, peasants and oppressed people in the most desperate of fight backs against the rich and powerful, see Unions as the only credible means of creating a better life for themselves their families and communities. The ruling classes of these countries likewise recognise the potential threat posed to their privileges by such grass roots organisations. In some countries, far from expecting a big car and seat at the table of the rich, union leaders expect only a short term of office before the ultimate sacrifice is made at the hands of the death squad or bosses hired killers. Many ordinary members of the unions face systematic repression and murder, yet still they retain their membership. Even in countries where unions are free to operate, legal attacks from governments and anti- union dirty tricks from employers seek to undermine union 'rights'.

Central African Republic: National Union of Central African Workers, struck, 1991 over pay and conditions. Strike leaders were imprisoned and union offices occupied by the police, six union federations banned.

Ethiopia: The new regime in 1991 suspended the leaderships of all Trade Unions, froze their assets and jailed many of them. It has effectively dismantled existing unions.

Mauritania: A complaint to the ILO's Committee On Freedom Of Association was brought by the Organisation Of African Trade Union Unity, it related to a two day general strike in June 91 called by the Mauritania TUC. It detailed information that Union leaders had been arrested and tortured, Interference by the government had led to the removal of its General Secretary and his replacements by a government puppet executive.

Sudan: Complaints from The World Federation Of Trade Unions and others related to measures taken by the military authorities after the coup of June 89, including dissolution of all Trade Unions, the imprisonment without charge of large numbers of Trade Unionists, the imposition of the death sentence by a military tribunal on two Union leaders and death under torture of a leading Trade Unionist.

Malawi: Highlighted by Amnesty for its infamous repression of trade unionists. One in particular Chakufwa Chihana General Secretary of the African Trade Union Co-ordination Council. He was arrested on his return from neighbouring Zambia after attempting to make a speech.

Lesotho: Use of internal security act to repress the Congress of Democratic Unions. Particularly Bank employees and teachers.

Kenya: Failure to allow emergence of free Trade Unions refusal to allow unions to register, and proscription of others particularly the strategic Timber Workers, Unions are further prevented from forming Federations.

Philippines: Unions particularly the militant ones such as Kilusang Mayo Uno (KMU) are targets for severe repression, including arbitrary arrests and charges, the killing of 11 KMU leaders during strikes in 1990 and the execution of two workers in march 92 during a Union demonstration.

Latin America: Bears the brunt of wide-ranging repression, torture and killing. Topping the list were Colombia, Guatemala, Honduras, Puru, Panama, and El Salvador. One complaint about this latter brought by the International Confederation of Free Trade Unions, included the murder of officials, the disappearance of workers and attacks on Union premises. Another complaint from the National Trade Union Federation Of Salvadoran Workers there were charges that between Feb. 89 and Jan 1990 there had been 87 murders and disappearances of Trade Union Leaders, 971 arrests and detentions of trade unionists and workers and 56 attacks on Union premises.
"The pattern of deaths and death squad style killings of Trade Unionists active in labour disputes suggest that government forces continue to be involved in human rights violations." (Amnesty)

Guatemala: Complaints to the ILO by the ICFTU concern murders, death threats and other forms of serious intimidation against Trade Union officials and discrimination against strikers, since January 1991 until May 93 there had been 15 murders of Union leaders 58 arrests nine death threats and a series of abductions and attacks.

Honduras: Complaints by the ICFTU and the United federation of Workers of Honduras concern the murders of Trade Union leaders Javier Banilla Medina and Ramon Antonia Briceno and threats on the lives of trade unionist Hilario Aguilera and his family. and the forced entry into his home by armed death squads. Another recent death that of Jesus Arieta Guerra Secretary general of the Rural Workers Union again blamed on state security forces.

Peru: A complaint by the World Confederation Of Organisations of the Teaching Profession included a series of murders and attacks upon members of the Peruvian Education Workers

Union (SUTEP) during the 1991 strike. The Peruvian General Confederation of Workers and others complained about the detention and disappearance of trade union leaders following the dissolution of parliament in 92.

Panama: Three complaints made by ICFTU and a number of Panamanian unions include allegations of mass dismissals in the public sector and seizing of union offices by the army.

Colombia: According to the National Teachers Union 53 teachers were killed in 91 and more than 400 issued death threats.

Middle East: Trade Unions face sever restrictions in Arab Asia, with Bahrain, Oman, Qatar, Saudi Arabia and United Arab Emirates banning Unions altogether.

The above information comes from Labour Research, May '93. The complete article includes reports on China, as well as the English speaking world.

Box 1: Top company donors to Conservative funds

There were 13 donations of £50,000 or more to the Conservative Party

Company	Donation £
Wittington Investments	150,000
Hambros	104,000
Hanson	100,000
P&O	100,000
Forte	82,000
Robert Fleming	75,000
Glaxo	60,000
Caledonia Investments	57,500
Tomkins	52,000
Sun Alliance	50,000
Guardian Royal Exchange	50,000
Scottish & Newcastle	50,000
Caledonian Mining	50,000

Box 2: Corporate donations traced by Labour Research as a proportion of overall donations to the Conservative Party

Financial year ending	Conservative Party donations figure (1) £000	Labour Research donations figures (2) £000	(2) as a %age of (1) %
March 1989	6,718	3,479	51.8
March 1990	7,090	3,815	53.8
March 1991	10,556	3,772	35.7
March 1994	9,372	2,837	30.3
March 1995	12,729	2,462	19.3

Appendix 2

Indiscipline and Rebellion in the 18th, 19th & 20th Century Coalfields

Disciplines and new behaviour patterns aspired to, by the industrial revolution were never really settled. There is a view that in-discipline, defiance, retention of the old ways & bursts of rebellion quickly burned out and where superseded by the relentless wheel of the industrial process. The reality is, new rhythms, new disciplines, in contrast to the old freedoms of the pre- industrial age were in many cases never finally settled, and are certainly in dispute well into the late C20th and in a number of ways still are.

While Hobsbawm recognises the riot on the 1700s and early 1800s as a form of collective bargaining, industrial relations of another means, it is wrong to suggest that this form of response was superseded by "*proper* Trade Unionism, and *organised* strikes".

Indeed in some industries which carried communities of people with it through time and the evolution of processes, such as mining and to a lesser extent the docks and among seafarers, there literally and not figuratively, was the passing on of the trade and skill, generation on generation and along with it chronicles of oral history, of class conflicts many generations long.

It seems odd that while this is readily accepted in patriotic notions of nations and nationality it is thought fanciful in the case of class; a more profound identity in my view. Yet with the continuation of skill came also the legacy of struggle, and riot was a weapon the miners would be very reluctant to lay down as we witnessed in the 1600s, 1700s and 1800s through to 1912 when troops were dispatched to the riotous coalfields and deployed at collieries, in 1920 companies of armoured cars sent to Scotland, York and Worcester, two infantry battalions and a battleship sent to Liverpool, tanks deployed to the northern coalfields, 1921 war office recalls troops from Ireland, Malta, Egypt, Palestine and Silesia. State of emergency called, Emergency Powers Act passed banning coal exports and horse racing! 1926 General Strike in support of the miners, gun boats, tanks and troops. 72, 73 and 74 the state moves in dark corners of surveillance, special forces and dirty tricks, but cannot prevent mass picketing, power cuts, a three day week, the collapse of a government and outright victory for the miners.

My book Pit Sense Versus The State reflecting in part on the 1984-85 strike, starts with an almost mirror image review of Doncaster pit villages in 1926. At the self same locations our grandparents fought in almost the same ways, with bricks and bats, and stones, and overturning vehicles, felling trees, setting up barricades against mounted police and baton charges and mass arrests. The book is in part dedicated to one aud lad who literally was involved in both struggles 58 years apart, as well as the struggles of 69-72 and 74 and a thousand pit rag-ups in between.

In '84-85 MacGreggor the Coal Board boss and Union buster complained that this was no longer a strike but an insurrection.

Ah well, insurrection as my old marra used to say "is a thing a dinnet care to speak aboot".

Although the radical response of the miners to the oppression of the owners and the state was similar everywhere, most of my examples come from me native Tyneside, because these are most familiar to is, both as oral history learned at the knee, but also in terms of systematic research and enquiry.

Before the dawn of the nineteenth century the coal industry was already quite large, certainly THE MOST concentrated accumulations of industrial workers in sprawling unorganised bothys found anywhere, conditions portrayed in Germinal were very similar to those endured by mining communities this side of the channel. Where they communities? I think its safe to say that the trade, the skill, the development of a distinct group of workers, following each other generation upon generation into the mines had been a process already 400 or 500 year long, particularly in the coal counties Northumberland, Durham, Scotland, parts of Yorkshire, the Midlands etc. A consistent core of mining families often relocating from one coal county to another developed in many places almost like ethnic groups. Of course following your father and grandfather into the pit wasn't always a choice and in Scotland the bond bound all children born of miners to the mine owner a practice which had died out elsewhere in Britain and in the USA slavery formally was abolished before the injustice was redressed in Scotland, and in Northumberland and Durham where the bond was for twelve months at a time and only applied to men and boy children.

The great struggles of the early nineteenth century on Tyneside, the emergence of first regional and then confederated national miners unions were to centre on this issue.

The existence of the bond, must not be seen as evidence that resistance was crushed, far from it, strikes and more particularly riot and sabotage was a major factor in eighteen and early nineteenth century mining communities. The keelmen a distinct group of riverboat sailors and rowers inseparably linked to the miners, seemed to have a unwritten nostrum that there wasn't much point having a strike unless it was accompanied with rebellion. Gateshead Parish Church has records of "keelmen's mutinees" in 1671 so they were well practised at it.

At a time when atheism was severely punished these communities were openly hostile and irreligious. When John Wesley came with missionary zeal to urge them all to repent, they attacked him and made to throw him in the river. In 1739-40 during a bitterly hard winter and a poor harvest, the grain merchants withdrew supplies in order to force prices even higher, in under six months the price of rye and wheat, the staple food of the poor rose by 160% as the poor died in droves. Pamela Armstrong in an excellent little history of 'the toon', tells us more. On the 9th June the keelmen and pitmen liberated a grain ship and distributed its cargo. They marched on accompanied by the poor of the quayside to the Guildhall, where their way was found to be blocked by a body of militiamen. As the crowd surged forward, a gun was discharged and a boy fell dead. The crowds fell momentarily silent then a great roar of anger burst forth as the crowd charged and dispersed the militia, The gentlemen of the Corporation, mostly merchants themselves, retreated behind the locked doors of the Guildhall. Mayor Fenwick described the scene "stones flew in among us like cannon shot..at length the mob broke in on us" though their lives were saved the building was trashed, and the toon hutch, or treasure trove was taken, its funds distributed in good order according to need. Meantime the city was in the hands of the rioters, and old scores were being settled, the militiamen taking refuge in their barracks, while the city gentlemen were "escorted" back to their homes by the mocking ranks of the poor. The prisoners were all released from jail amid much huzzaing and blowing of horns, and the shopkeepers were forced to lower the prices to more reasonable levels. The pitmen were are told "marched in great order through the town with bagpipes playing, drums beating and dirty clothes fixed upon sticks by way of colours flying". By the time troops of cavalry had assembled from Morpeth and Alnwick the crowds had gone to their beds happy that some injustice at least had been addressed.

This is not the pamphlet in which to discuss, the ethnicity of the Tynesider and folk of Northumbria, except to say that stout efforts have been made by historians to suppress widespread evidence since the time of the Angle invasion, of resistance to Angle absorption and ethnic cleansing of the native Celtic peoples. Often this has taken the form of "my enemies enemy is my friend" firstly in a welcome embrace to the Vikings, then later in virtually every Scottish / English clash, the good folk of Northumbria sides with the Scots. In the Civil war, the city merchants & coal barons, the Newcastle Hostmen see the political yardage in the capitalist revolution, and bide within the City walls, the miners join the army of the Scots to blow them up.

Later the 1714 Jacobite rebellion seen the famous Earl of Derwentwater from his castle in Bamburgh join the Scots forces, while The Castle at Lindsfarne was one of the last to stand in support of that cause, the rebellion, though everywhere ignored by historians continued in Northumberland through the 1720s at least. I had gained knowledge of this initially from the messages of the prisoners scratched for all to see on the dungeon walls of Bamburgh castle, after it had fallen to George, and clearly visible right into the 1970s until some pillock decided to make alterations to accommodate tourists and in the process had the walls replastered!

The position of the English garrison at its northern outpost in the City earned us the title Geordies, supporters of the southern king, it was a clear misnomer. Even four years *after* the bloody suppression of the 1745 rebellion the miners and keelmen marched in rebellion to Elswick to declare Tyneside "no longer part of a kingdom ruled by an imported German Monarch ... they declared that Charles Stuart was the true and recognised king of Newcastle" what the position of the coal and river communities had been *during* the rebellion we are never told, there seems a conspiracy of silence that awkward rebellions against kings, and even nationality should not be explored, this interesting diversion is one in great need of in depth research.

The seamen were in determined struggle against conscription in the 1790s against conditions endured when pressed into service in 1793 and wage conditions the year before. Pamela Armstrong in her Dark Tales of Old Newcastle tells us the efforts of the communities to repel the press gangs:-"If the press gangs could be lured into the warren-like maze of Sandgate the hunters would soon become hunted. At a pre-arranged signal, men women and children would spring out from concealment and pelt the press men with all manner of missiles, If caught, the press men would be in for a severe beating before being subject to public ridicule and humiliation. The men were marched through Sandgate with their jackets turned inside out and their officers obliged to 'ride the steng'- a tiny seat attached to the end of a long pole on to which the unfortunate officer would be strapped and : *carried through the streets exposed to the insults and assaults of an enraged populace, the women in particular bedaubing them plentifully with dirt etc.* " (Newcastle Journal 23 April 1760). The keelmen of Tyne and Wear were in joint action together with the seamen in 1793, then again on the Tyne in 1794; then another anti conscription strike ten years later and against price rises in 1809. Amid the turmoil of 1793 the mines of the counties turned out, by 1810 it was the Bond that the centre piece of Miners union strike action. Robert Colls describes the situation "for a period in 1793 the Tyne was in a situation of a general strike. Traditional labour action on the river was not content with a withdrawal of labour. Protest usually took the form of *direct* confrontation and exercises of power; the seamen would seize the river and control daily sailing's according to their demands, the keelmen would blockade the river or sabotage its facilities, whilst the pitmen were infamous for commando attacks on colliery machinery ..."

In 1794 the Tyne keelmen destroyed the coal stathes which threatened their bargaining power and skills, whilst the year before hundreds of armed seamen, with cutlass's and pistols attacked *The Eleanor* a Royal navel ship on board of which conscripted comrades were held. In that year the three groups together with the broad populace refused to pay taxes, and resisted any attempts to collect them.

The end of the Napoleonic war brought a new wave of revolutionary activism, with an insurrection of the keelmen on the Wear a wave of colliery and seamen's strikes on the Tyne in 1815. The new stathes were destroyed, whilst the seamen captured the river. The staiths were a piece of emerging technology aimed at displacing the Keels and the keel bullies, the men had recognised the impending danger one hundred and ten years earlier when the first of the anti staith strikes hit the river. A year later the Sunderland miners led a grain riot. Almost every year seen radical determined and often armed action by the workers. A permanent enforcement of the riot act was required and in 1792 The Hon Captain Cochrane, with the HMS Hind was dispatched to the river however it wasn't long before the real source of authority was demonstrated and on 20th Nov. he reports to the Home Office.
"Upon my arrival at Shields I found everything on shore perfectly quiet the seamen every-where behaving with the utmost degree of civility and regularity except that they made the point to board all the ships that sailed to satisfy themselves that the crew had not broke the General (wage) Agreement"
 In the coalfields of the seventeen hundreds the spirit of rebellion together with what the authorities deemed drunken and sexual abandon & the absence of any moral constraints mortified bourgeois society and ensured the regular presence of troops and frequent deployment of marines to quell the industrial and general urban riots.

One of the most famous incidents became known as the Peterloo Massacre in 1819, when mounted Yeomanry (in practice armed Tory volunteers) sabres flaying indiscriminately rode into a crowd of 80,000 who had gathered to protest at the repeal of the Corn Laws. At least 11 died and several hundred were seriously injured.

It polarised the nation. At once the Town Council of Newcastle sent a message of congratulations to the Prince Regent and promised to deal with "the forces of anarchy and atheism in Newcastle". The "atheists and Anarchists" thought differently and the whole of Tyneside rose in protest. They marched from all corners of Northumberland and Durham, banners flying, bands playing. We are told, "the societies marched four abreast, arms linked, their leaders bearing white rods crowned with crape. Banners bore the words Truth, Order, Justice, & quoting the radical poet Robert Burns "We'll be brothers for a' that". The bands played 'Scots wh' ha'e', the adopted anthem of the Tyneside radicals and later the Northern Chartists, while others seen no contradiction in playing Rule Britannia as a confrontational challenge to the armed forces of Britannia.

It should be noted that many of the radicals aspired to some unspecified notion of a free country, caught, they thought, in the words of such songs. The ruling class and their forces were not 'true' Englishmen, the state defiled the free sons of the waves characterised in the song.

Scots wh' ha'e or Rule Britannia, 80,000 gathered on the Town Moor and passed resolutions protesting "The outrage at Manchester". Claiming "the rights and liberties of Englishmen", they denounced Tyranny and Oppression. It is not known how many of the crowd were armed, though many certainly were; the military stayed away. The Mayor of Newcastle wrote to the Home Secretary Viscount Sidmouth, six days following the meeting :-
It is impossible to contemplate the meeting of the 11th inst. without awe, more especially if my information is correct, that 700 of them were prepared with arms (concealed) to resist the civil powers. These men came from a village about three miles from this town; and there is strong reason to suspect that arms are manufactured there; they are chiefly forgemen.

Of course it was to the revolutionary men of Winlaton he was referring. The forge at Winlaton, still standing by the way but it seems the local populace have now forgotten what it is, was at the very apex of the industrial revolution, it was also famous for supplying men and arms for the political revolution, among other to the communards of the Paris Commune.

The Winlaton insurrectionists were popularly known at Crowley's crew (after their work place) and were well armed. They had manufactured pikes in large numbers and primitive hand grenades, but also the lethal effective caltrop, in dialect "Craa foot" four pronged instruments when however thrown land with one spike up, and ready to crippled a cavalry horse. Frank Graham, correctly in my view, suggests:-

"These stern measures of the Winlaton men made a repetition of Peterloo impossible in Newcastle, and on many other occasions the presence of "Crowleys Crew" prevented interference by the authorities."

We are told in the political ferment of those times Newcastle and surrounding towns teemed with pamphlets, and tracts, on the question of Reform, petitions, placards and a tide of political protest marked the region.

Sometimes even the best attempts of the ruling class to mollify the populace, as during the coronation of George 1V in 1821 came to grief. The canons fired from the castle keep, the bells from Newcastle's churches and cathedral rang out and the city had been laid open for a grand celebration. Robert Colls tells us what happened:-
"At 9.30 a.m. the Mayor and Corporation read a congratulatory address to the king, and George Foster was invested with the gold chain and medallion of office, where upon the whole party marched in procession to St Nicholas for a coronation service." Meantime outside things were taking an odd turn, a gang of women had hoisted an effigy of the rival queen Caroline, a favourite with the town's people. The mail coaches coming into the town covered in ribbons were given rough passage through the crowd.

The Corporation in honour of the day had erected three beer tents and one fountain which flowed wine, called 'a pant', two oxen had been slaughtered and had been getting cooked since the previous evening.

Of course as the wine began to flow the teeming masses of the quayside struggled to be within its tide, a sailor climbed up the fountain on top of which was a crown on a throne, torn down the crown amid cheers and sat himself in the throne atop the flowing claret. This turned out to be an envied position and with some considerable difficulty the man almost stripped naked was removed from the throne, in a sort of debauched and hysterical king of the castle game. The Tyne Mercury informs us "Several seamen, pitmen keelmen and others were at different times mounted on the roof of the pant".

The butchers who had been employed to slice the oxen meat and throw it into the crowd, found themselves being pelted back by lumps of meat. Next the roasting spits were overturned and the carcasses paraded through the streets, on route the mail coaches were attacked by stone throwing crowds who then attacked the Yeomanry. Their commander, Thomas Burdon who had been knighted for his actions against the rebellious Tyne seamen in 1815 took flight on this occasion. As soon as the wine fountains had run dry they were smashed up, a bit like the custom of throwing vodka glasses in the fire place, only on a bigger scale. Then the cities windows took the brunt of the merriment, Cole tells us "wildness increased until mercifully for the Corporation all was stifled by mid-afternoon with an exodus to the Town Moor for the races". The riot came to explained in many ways, it had been an alcoholic bribe to win the loyalty of rebellious people, the casting of meat to the crowds like favours to a dog, and other such insults lit a spark, for others it was just the presence of the boose, along with a goodly collection of Town big wigs and fat cats, reason enough to change the days agenda. Although a radical song of the period suggests:-

> "Blush ye great Rulers of the toon,
> Behold your nauseous loathsome boon
> See men, with manner more discreet,

Disgusted, spurn your beastly treat
And know, all you who term *us* swine
That *reason* rules the sons of Tyne."

Between 1791 and 1815 the Northumbrian and Durham coalfield and broadly those based around the Tyne enjoyed a boom period, the pitmen and their ancillary brothers on the keels and elsewhere had endured a strong bargaining position, partly through the shortage of man-power due to the Napoleonic war, and the need to expand industrial production. Not for the last time in history would the miners be outside of the patriotic war efforts in support of their own class positions. The need of the state to enforce the regions sailors and keelers into the navy met with pitched battles on a number of occasions and the 'Geordies' refused to follow the colours. In 1793 The Tyne royal navy crews struck, not against the war as such, but against the degradation and slave wages of the service Peter Rothes the impress officer for Newcastle reported to the admiralty that the law could not control the restless seamen or prevent their ceaseless parading and counter marching and their speechifying against the wages and conditions prevalent in His Majesty's service.

In 1818 happened what was locally called the Battle of Stanhope. In truth although miners were the archetypal proletarian, they were also often fields and fen men, poaching was a right, to be fought for if necessary. The Bishop of Durham thought otherwise and posted a notice of prosecution against all poachers. The miners of Weardale ignored it. At last in 1818 an army of the Bishops men, heavily armed came into the town to arrest two of the best known of the hunters. They were taken to The Black Bull Inn. News of the arrest and the invaders quickly spread and soon an army of armed miners were on the scene. Frank Graham tells us:
"a large crowd gathered, and a fierce battle broke out. The Bishop's men were completely routed. Many keepers and constables were severely injured and the Inn floor was covered in blood."

A song of the period, (interestingly to a Jacobite lament) records:-

"So this army set out from high Oakland we hear,
H. Wye in the front and black bitch in the rear
On they marched to Wolsingham then made a halt
And concerning the battle began to consult.

They heard that the miners grand army was strong,
The captain that led them was full six foot long
That put Mr Wye in a bodily fear
And back to great Oakland he wish'd for to steer.

Up spoke the game keepers "Cheer up never fear"
Through Stanhope and Weardale our way we will clear
In Durham or Oakland it shall never be said
That by a few miners our army was paid

So the army set off straightaway as we hear
And the miners grand army did quickly appear
Oh they fired along till their powder was done
And then they laid on with the butt-end of their gun

They dismounted the riders straightaway on the plain
H Wye and black bitch in the battle were slain
Oh they that ran fastest got first out of town
And away they went home with their tails hanging down

Oh this bonny moor hen, she has feathers anew
She has many fine colours but none of them blue
Oh the miners of Weardale they are all valiant men
They will fight till they die for the bonny moor hen.

The 1815-20 period was one of mass political uprising in all the major industrial centres of Britain and the state wet its collective britches with fears of working class insurrection and the riotous mob. 1822 seen the last great battle (called "The lang stop") between the keelmen and the coalowners with the backing of state forces, to install the staiths and displace their labour. The strike was accompanied with great violence, pitched battles ensued at North Shields, Scotswood and in the Castle Garth. The army and Royal Navy were rushed in, and the battleship SWAN was moored in the river, the guns pointed menacingly at Sandgate and ever ready to rake the quay with cannon shot. Police and specials patrolled the streets and large numbers of the military were drafted in. Seven ships of the line lay in Shields harbour to quell the strike. As usual in the strikes of the pitmen or keelmen the river's seamen came to the assistance of their brothers and joined the rising. Despite the fearful array of armed bodies of men and equipment the river was blockaded by the seamen in solidarity with the keel boulies, the coal trade ground to a halt and London's merchants began to look to other sources of fuel, the first real threat to the Hostmen's monopoly in centuries.. Attempts by marines to sail the keels themselves were calamitous, and eventually the only boats they were able to sail were towed by a contraption modified from a steam engine and fitted with paddles to replace its wheels. These vessels were also attacked both from the river and the banks, such that notices were posted throughout the area

"The Civil Authorities regret to find the deluded Keelmen continue to insult HIS MAJESTY's BOATS by throwing stones when protecting those that are willing to work; and finding forbearance any longer will endanger THE LIVES of those so employed,- This is to caution the peaceable inhabitants and women and children to keep within their houses during the time the keels are passing from the staiths to Shields, as the Marines have orders to fire on the first man that shall dare to throw a stone at them."

It always strikes me as a delightful picture, "excuse me sa, were the Royal Navy stop throwing stones!" "Get to fu..!" Armstrong paints us in a little more "The *Tom and Jerry* unused to its present task was temperamental and breakdowns were frequent. The keelmen would then gleefully wade out into the river and overturn the keels, tipping both coal and military guards into the water". After two months of the most bitter struggle, the steady trickle of coal breaking the blockade (and in comparison to normal export figures it was *a trickle)* the Keelmen were forced to return to work on point of starvation without securing guarantees on their trade. By 1876 the keelers as a class force for "atheism and anarchy" were virtually extinct.

Between 1830-31 The ruling class trembled as a whole series of local insurrection swept the country. In the cradle of bourgeois culture Otmoor in Oxfordshire seen masses of people from all over the county "possessing" the moors, tearing down enclosures and reclaiming the land and their own. Soon "Captain Swing" was in action all over the agricultural heartland's of southern and eastern England. A Sussex magistrate termed them "parochial insurrections". Raph Samuel a libertarian Communist historian and expert on the period tells us "the country bore a tumultuous appearance" At Nottingham The Duke of Newcastle's Castle was burned to the ground; At Derby the goal was sacked and the prisoners liberated. At Bristol the Mansion House, The Bishops Palace, The Custom House, three goals and "The best house in Queens Square" were destroyed. Samuel says "The Industrial movements bore the character of full scale social upheavals rather than of limited strikes. The striking miners of North Wales fought a battle with the military at Chirk Bridge. The Merthyr rioters disarmed the soldiery at one point in the rising and put the Yeomanry to flight. The cotton strike in Southeast Lancashire was marked by huge demonstrations, and turn out marchings from town to town; it also produced one of the famous industrial murders of the 19th Century - the assassination of Thomas Ashton, the master cotton spinner of Hyde, shot down by a party of men (one of them a travelling wizard!) on January 3rd 1831".

The disturbances spreading from farming districts in the South and east to the mining and manufacturing districts of North Wales, the Black Country, Lancashire, Tyneside and West Cumberland. "Colliers were showing turbulent disposition in Staffordshire; they were holding threatening meetings in County Durham. There were general strikes in the North Wales coalfield and in the cotton towns of south-east Lancashire; whilst in the South rick-burning and incendiarism were following in the wake of Swing." (Raph Samuel, Forward: Class Struggle in 19th Century Oxfordshire, by Bernard Reaney)

By May and June armed rebellions often led my miners were developing in a number of places, notably in the Forest of Dean where "The Free Miners Of Dean" rose against enclosures. At Merthyr Tydfil the miners and ironworkers seized and held the town against armed Yeomanry. By Autumn the captain had reached the cities, where riots greeted the Reform Bill crisis. Whilst it is true that the nationwide insurrections were grist to the mill of the Political Unionists, they were not *part* of that political process. The riots, the burnings, the shootings, the possessions were about working class people taking back the framework of society and production not about rotten boroughs. As Raph Samuel says:- *"The commoners of Otmoor provide good example. They did not wait upon the tedious processes of representation and the law, which had already cheated them out of their land; they repossessed the land themselves, and put the entire paraphernalia of the enclosers work to the axe."*

The Cathedral towns of Canterbury and Exeter seen bishops burned in effigy on Guy Fawkes day. Samuel goes on:

"Gaols were attacked in Derby and Preston, and at Nottingham the Castle. Reform rioters in Worcester fought with constables, beating them into retreat and pelting troops of the 7th Hussars with stones. The Bath mob rose to prevent the cavalry making off for Bristol." In Bristol itself the riots which broke out on the evening of October 29th were described as having the character of an urban jacquerie, with "the scum of the quays and the collieries" and likened to The Gorden riots of fifty years earlier.

The insurrectionists were at times given to dressing in women's clothes and adopting a female title, most famous of these perhaps, courtesy of Hollywood, were the Molly Maguires. That the female dress disguised the identity of the saboteur or assassin was a feature of the practice but it was more than that, it was part of a much more ancient custom toasting a reversal of roles. An up with all that is down, a world turned upside down, the men as women, the poor as the rich, the children as adults, the adult as child, the powerless as powerful. The Luddites were just such costumed crusaders, and in the northern pits the vengeful combatant was called Rebeckah, as I believe she was in Wales.

"Thomas Johnson, Castle Eden Colliery.
We are informed that you have started to brake a standing engine at Castle Eden on the 15th of April 1844. Therefore as I have the honner to be the Mother of so numerous a family I wish to take the opertunity of informing you of the danger that you are standing in, and you know not how soon the result may be. As you know that youre felow workmen has joined the Union (and you have taken there plases) therefore take notice that if you remain as you are you may rest ashoured that at an houre when you think not that your liffe will be demanded in such a manner as you think not if you are inclined to live a little longer you must JOIN THE UNION as soon as posable and be a man in the land of freedom.
              Signed on Behalph, mis Cromewel and your Leage Ladey
                                    Rebeckah From The Mountains."

Colls says "Rebeckah moved quickly and always at night: windows would shatter, doors would burst open, and the grotesque sight of men in women's clothes, their faces blackened and revenging would confront you. Wallsend suffered severe visits in the June of 1844, and so did a score of other collieries during the spring and summer. The terror may have been mercurial in action, but the impression is of superb planning. Thomas Wood to Rowland Burton wrote of the Thornley attacks "The Colliers were very violent and well organised, and they kept up a continual system of terror ... watching their houses at night, issuing threatening placards of "Rebecca visits" going about in Women's clothes etc ..."

It was during this period that the fearful ode to *The Blackleg Miners* was composed:

> Oh, Deleval is a terrible place
> they rub wet clay in the blacklegs face
> and aroond the heap they run a foot race
> With the dorty black-leg miners.

Divind gaan near the Seghill mine
for across the Way they've stretched a line
to catch the throat and smash the spine
of the dorty black-leg miners

They'll tek ya duds and tools as well
and hoy ye doon that pit o'hell
Doon ye gaan and fair-thee-well
Thou dorty black-leg miner

So join the Union while ye may
deant wait till ya dyin day-
for THAT may not be far away
Thou dorty black-leg miner!

In the struggles of Hepburn's regional union, of the 1830,s imported blacklegs from Stafford-shire and Wales were mercilessly hounded by the whole native populace. Feb. 1833 the battles were widespread throughout the county but at Wideopen the ferociousness reached levels only previously seen at Seghill, pokers and fire irons some of them red hot were used to dissuade the strike and union breakers.

"Job Davies, a Welshman, rushed from his home only to be confronted by a woman brandish-ing a poker (this was a real woman not a dressed up miner) the next he knew he was down and bleeding only to wake up the next morning on the slag heap of West Moor pit, a quarter of a mile away."

The first successful endeavour to found a national mineworkers Union came in the 1840s in the midst of the general revolutionary upsurge. The world's first working class "party", if we can call it that, in the shape of The Chartists, was born, and cheek by jowel so too was The Miners Association, the world's first industrial Union. From their inception both were intrin-sically linked in revolutionary vision and radical struggle. Many of the Chartist leaders were also leaders of the Miners Union. Chartism encapsulated radical social reformers as well as violent revolutionaries, a movement for civil rights having within its ranks the early commu-nist visionaries who saw political reform as inseparably linked to the radical transformation of society in the form of economic justice for working people.

The coal owners were the haughty land-owning aristocrats who made a fortune in the indus-trial revolution. The British Empire itself came to rest on coal and on the point of the collier's pick. Among the most notable coal owners were Lord Longsdale, Lord Londonderry, Earl Fitzwilliam, The Countess of Durham, Lord Joicey, The Marquess of Bute, Lord Lambton, Lord Bradford and the Earl of Balcarres. Such people were outraged that so vital and numer-ous a body as the miners were being won not only to trade unionism, but to revolutionary ideology as well. The great Geordie miners leader Martin Jude was a member of the General Council of the Chartist movement, The North East coalfield was in fact a stronghold of the physical force wing on the movement. Augustus Beaumont published his Northern Liberator

from Newcastle Upon Tyne, castigating the moderates:
"Those men were fed and therefore relied on moral force, but let them labour for one week and be ill fed and ill clothed and it would soon convert their moral force to physical force".

Julian Harney, writing in the winter of 1838-39, found the atmosphere in the pit villages exhilarating:-
"In small villages out from Newcastle the exhortation to arms was being taken quite literally ... fowling pieces, small cannon, stoneware grenades, pikes and "craa,s feet" or caltrops ... were being turned out in quantities. It was localities like this, which on hearing rumours that troops would be present at the great meeting in Newcastle on Christmas day, sent couriers to find out if they were to bring arms with them."

We are told by Raymond Challinor in his "History of The Miners Association" that miners' banners in those days bore inscriptions like "He that hath no sword, let him sell his shirt and buy one".

In a strange premonition of the "armalite and the ballot box" strategy, Julian Harney at the frequent Northumbrian and Durham rallies urged the crowd to "carry a musket in one hand and a petition in the other". In the national miners' strike of 1844, while a company of the 37 Regiment and two troops of 8th Hussars were in readiness in Newcastle the Newcastle, Courant reported, "The women assumed as offensive a position as that taken by their husbands and indeed more reckless of the consequences," whilst in Lancashire Welsh colliers brought in to scab were met by a force of 1,000s of strikers, who, The Manchester Guardian reports:-
"assailed them with stones, brickbats and other missiles, severely hurting some of the police."

1848 was a year of revolutions throughout Europe, in Britain The Miners seemed the force most likely to bring around ours, An enormous meeting of Scottish miners in Airdrie soon after the revolution in France addressed by a local revolutionary miner called Lee declared the evils befalling the working class were due to political inequalities and warned the capitalists and aristocracy to beware the impending workers' insurrection.

Five years later striking Lancashire colliers seized the city of Wigan. After eight weeks of rioting, Challinor says:
"The police discreetly barricaded themselves in the police station, they were only released when a troop of cavalry rode from Preston and with the use of what was called 'severe repression' restored 'law and order'."

One of the great revolutionary leaders at the end of the seventeen hundreds was Tommy Hepburn, founder of the United Miners of the 1830s and an outstanding Chartist activist. Although that Union was entirely broken and he himself was blacklisted throughout the counties and reduced to selling tea to stay alive, he stormed back onto the political stage in 1838 as one of the founders of "The Working Men's Association". This organisation was primarily an alliance of radical forces trying to end the Poor Law. When Victoria was crowned they held what we are told was "a monster republican demonstration with 400 banners and 40 bands". Later that year the Northern Political Union was formed to fight for the peoples charter, Hepburn was one of its most dynamic leaders. Our early revolutionary coal mining forebears left and indelible mark upon our industry and the character of our Unions as they developed. It proved impossible, despite the development of hefty and at times right wing bureaucracies, and social democratic political currents, to remove. One only awaited a new upsurge of miners militancy to scratch the surface, and the old insurrectionist incendarist saboteur took shape like Morrisons ghosts of the dead Indians, the image and courage of the past ran on again alongside a new insurgent generation as we will demonstrate in the following chapter Things That Go Bump In the Night.

Taking a different aspect *lacking* Hobsbawm's references to St Monday, the tradition of laying idle the work place in the early days of industrialisation and before the discipline of the clock took firm hold, misses the fact that that St was respected right through C19 and C20 mining communities, and neither iconoclastic Union pragmatists, War effort supporting Communists, or steely eyed Coal Board production managers were able to root it out until the industry was smashed to a shadow in '92-93. Even the monumental defeat of 1984-85 and management's attempts at imposing new disciplines failed. In the mid '80s we find production managers lambasting Union leaders about absences of up to 20% on Mondays at many Doncaster pits, and that even the deputies, front line supervisors were almost as bad as the men. The now famous mass face to face meeting of the Doncaster Area production manager Mr Tregelis with the entire 2,000 strong compliment of Bentley miners, at which he led with his chin, with the question "Why do you only work four shifts per week" to which many in chorus replied "Because we can't live on three". In the late '60s when there was work outside mining, and men came and went several times a year so threats of the sack just didn't connect, men sometimes did in fact live on three, particularly missing the Monday day shift because of boozing Sunday night and missing Friday afters or nights because it interfered with the weekend's boozing.

In the period roughly covered by Zola's excellent description and virtually into the mid-1860s, the seasons and ancient holidays impacted harder than the clock, which was only during times of utmost collapse of trade or the union able to force out the ancient customs. There were in the northern coalfields times of the year when men and boys refused to work; there were no women in the Northumbrian and Durham coalfields, probably because heavy capital investment in the form of the gallowa or pit pony had either replaced them sometime preceding the mid 1600s or else had pre-empted their employment; although this presumption of mine can only be partly true since the gallowa didn't oust the young laddies hand putting until the 1940s and the two worked in conjunction. This was not the case in Scotland, nor it seems any of the other coalfields where women and girls worked doing the work of ponies, and even after they were excluded from underground work, continued to labour on the pit brow, I believe until the beginning of the 1950s in Lancashire. It might be noted that it was the moral outrage of the Victorian middle class drawing room, and the hypocrisy of all sorts of religious sky pilots who eventually got the women and girls out of the mines, not we hasten to add because of the back breaking toil, the death, disease and injury, but the nakedness and sexual promiscuity which the rich and comfortable in their cosseted lifestyles *imagined* was going on in the dark heat of the mine. I say *imagined* because while ever it is doubtless true the lack of an age bar on premature death, crippling disease, and injury together with merciless toil would render an age bar on sexual activity quite pointlessly stupid, and that people who think their final moment might come at any day will not hold back from the few free pleasures the good lord had bequeathed upon their person, but rather because it would take a lustful pair of individuals indeed to take time off from pushing massive trams of coal across awkward, roadways on their hands and knees through waste deep water and clouds of dust, to have a quick shag and then resume their labours.

However I digress! These unofficial holidays (what an absurd idea, that someone else should say when you can take a day off) these labourless days were kept as Gaudy days, days of colour, it could be the first day a cuckoo was heard, the peas had reached maturity or some other crop had come of age, the obliging item then christened that particular day.

Thomas Wilson, writing in the 1840s, gives a poetic description of the holidays:-

> A cuckoo-morning give a lad
> He values out his plagues a cherry
> A Back or knowe myeks hewers glad
> A gaudy days myeks a hands merry.

130 odd years later I wrote, "In the summer months on afternoon shift, sun high in the sky, girls in their summer gear, me walking along dirty old pit bag slung over me shoulder ... one sees in the field a dozen or so lads, bait bags used as pillows, snap tins open and the contents being swigged down to the accompaniment of bottles of beer from the nearby pub. I ask, "picnicking?" "Aye, for a minute we thowt we'd get there." It was a close run thing, requiring only an invitation to share the contents of my sandwiches to produce another totally irresponsible cavalier response. The pit, after all, we were assured would be there tomorrow, but the sun might not.

An 18th Century visiting clergyman Eneas Mackenzies warns of these pitfolk at the Hoppins: "These dancing parties often exhibit scenes very indelicate and unpleasant to the peaceable spectator, with virility at stake and drink encouraging the virility. Midnight courting, connived at by the girls' parents, is no less shameless, but fathers have no notion of denying those under their care that indulgence which they themselves and their ancestors have practised with impunity before them."

Discipline

Despite the signing of the most reaching national industrial relations contract probably ever in the history of any British industrial enterprise, the National Power Loading Agreement signed in 1967, heralding official national union compliance with Supervision of miners, particularly face workers was bitterly resented, and as the late '60s passed into late '70s it was frankly ignored. Carter Goodrich talking of a case arising under the Minimum Wages Act in the early part of this century tells of an Overman's called to give evidence to the court and say whether a certain worker did his job properly. The overman answered that he didn't know. "I never saw him work". The magistrate insisted "but isn't it your duty under the Mines Act to visit each working place twice a day?" "Yes" came the reply. "Then why" said the magistrate "didn't you ever see him work?" To which the overman replied "they always stop work when they see an overman coming, and sit down till he's gone - they even take out their pipes if it's a mine free of gas. They won't let anybody watch them". This tradition was one which just would not die. Nor be killed. Another aspect of the failed disciplinary element (it had many strengths also) was the designation of all face workers as multi denominational Power Loaders, no longer stonemen, hewers, cutters or whatever. Writing of this in 1972 I observe "most of the separate tasks still exist on a power loaded face and workers remain of the self-same tasks ... Once they have a task, it is *their* task and nobody else's; once they have a unit it is their unit, once they have a particular skill nothing will budge them to perform someone else's. Today they continue to claim their own class of work regardless of the fact they are supposed now to be all as one. You may find the caunchmen arrive for work only to be told by the deputy at the Kist. "There's no work for you lads today. The face hasn't travelled far enough and there is no caunch to work." I should hasten to add that the men would suffer not the slightest loss of income by this eventuality and would simply fill in where needed on other work. Still the men would insist, eventually ignoring the deputy all together, refusing redeployment, board the manrider and ride into their normal place of work, and there by hook or by crook will construe a way of find their own class of work. Should the deputy attempt to deploy the spare caunchmen, stoneworkers to the coal nueks or stables, they will insist that all spare colliers, the men who work the coal as such, be deployed there first. Failure to do so has stopped innumerable coalfaces and even whole collieries. It was always seen as a thin wedge inserted to break the workers control of deployment and manning and rob us of are ancient skills.

Disputes rarely ever could get settled on a Friday even when the original irritant had gone. In 1989 A big vociferous electrician Steve Clarkson from the nearby Brodsworth colliery had been off on the sick before the start of the colliery holidays and so didn't see the notice which said the lockers were going to be cleaned out. When he returned to work after the holidays he found his rags had been thrown out, along with his industrial glasses. The loss of his industrial glasses caused him to kick and scream and eventually go home in disgust. "The useless wankers in the Union office said it was me own fault" he complained loudly every time he seen me in town. Finding this rather amusing I had relayed the story to a group of the lads down Hatfield pit as we eat wa baits. Months later I had occasion to turn up on a Friday night to tell the men in the canteen that the dispute which had stopped days and afters shift & was odds on to stop night shift too, was now *settled*, and they could go to work. This brought a stunned silence and men with utmost reluctance started to shuffle towards the lockers to get changed. Suddenly one shouts "What about Steve Clarkson's glasses then?" and at once the air was full of indignation at the truly vile treatment this comrade, never seen or heard of before, had been treated, the fact that he didn't work at our pit was matterless, tonight anyway, and off they streamed home or rather to the pub. The manager was mystified, and on hearing about the glasses cried "but I'll give him another set of glasses". "Well you can't" I explained, it was three months ago and anyway, he worked at Brodsworth twelve miles away.

Around the same period Bentley night shift wouldn't go down the pit because of cloudy water in the taps, they sat in the canteen and awaited an official of the Water Board hastily summoned by the Colliery manager, who came and sampled the water and tested it, declaring that it was just sediment and would anyway soon clear. So they sat, and sat, and sat, every so often the Night shift control overman coming back with a glass of water, holding it up to the assembled workforce and ask, that's clear now isn't it. "No" they would respond without question. Eventually the manager hit on an idea, it was now half way through the shift, they hadn't even got down the pit yet, but he'd pay them a full shift, and issue every man with four pints of orange juice from the canteen and bussed in from nearby collieries. Sounded good, they all queued up, got the orange juice, and either drank it then and there or else took it home for the young'uns, but they all went home anyway. When the following week came around the whole pit struck because the night shift had not been paid.

I think what is important to grasp is that this was a period following the biggest defeat of the miners since 1926, and in a time when no less than 100,000 jobs had gone in four years our incantation was both *no pit closures* and *but its not a job at any price*.

Old habits die hard. As industrial relations hit rock bottom at Hatfield in 1989 the wizards of the international business school Cooper and Lybrands were brought in to analyse the workforce and recommend changes, I later envisaged it as a pantomime for it was to become something of *the babes in the wood meet the bull in the china shop*. As a bouncy bright eyed business suited young women failed to see the massed ranks of large unshaven sullen miners staring in mystification as she went into her routine established on thoughtful quietly shirt sleeved office clerks "Who are we bringing to the party today then?"

The second of the sessions, aimed at the vital development teams, was to be presented at a local hotel, with Sunday dinner laid on for 30 miners. The men were to receive the Sunday double time payment and would thus draw the equivalent of a full days underground wage for sitting in the day light being told how to communicate. Headed *An Exercise In Communication* it had been called at 9am on a Sunday morning, wait a minute get up *before* 8am on a *Sunday* to exercise in communication after a long Saturday night boozing? £42? £100 wouldn't have made the slightest difference, turn over go back to sleep. Seven turned up much the worse for ware, although as the dinner was being served at 12.30 another six turned up just as the clock turned 12.30 "just to put their faces in" they said and of course sit down to the traditional Sunday dinner replete with Yorkshire puddings and gravy and to claim a full days wage for a splendid spread. The exercise in communication had failed to recognise long standing pit customs. Like wise their LIFO exercise, which involved filling in a multitude of question and answers to disclose psychological barriers to harmonious industrial and personal relations? Totally missing the miners skills at Pillock, or piss taking they never really understood the miners ability to work the answers backward, awarding themselves positively Franciscan qualities of harmony and consciousness behaviour styles. Only management, who were also to dutifully fill out the forms filled them truthfully emerging as absolute asocial nut cases who would best left isolated on a deserted island.

So too the question of conformity to automation and work process, of supervision and management control, readers of our (I wrote with Joel Krieger) book *A Miners Life* will see much evidence, of early miners skill and job control, of self supervision and team selection, of control over weekend manning and overtime work, staying firmly in the hands of the mines despite harsh attempts to take into managerial prerogative.

The great year long printers strike in Britain in '85-86 against new computer multi-operational terminals away from Fleet Street and new custom built premises at Wapping, was an ancient echo of shots first fired from the barrels of The Keelmen and then Luddism, centring on job controls, & specific craft skills against deskilling technical processes which passed power and direction away from operators and into the hands of management

The industrial revolution, was not at its inception anyway as some might perceive the move from labour intensive, hand work to labourless machine production. Raph Samuel's draws attention to the labour intensity engendered by industrialisation. This is solidly testified to by the late C20th coal industry, as we demonstrate in A Miners Life particularly page 18.

The years following the great coal strike of 84-85 were a watershed, with management at pit levels at first confused and divided as to what the objectives now were, some had thought the point was to get back on stream, more production. New strategies were being devised, systems analysis, delay analysis, flexible working, and a new species of contract. Overall the state's strategy was to take the still sizeable mining industry even after the closures following 85, drive the union out of it by breaking their authority with the workforce, bring in self motivating contracts, more carrot less stick, but deal direct with the men not the union, which will be frozen out of negotiations.

Now Arthur Scargill always says we didn't loose the '84 strike, which is just as well, because if what we'd been through was a victory I'd dread to think what would have happened if we had *really* lost. But the question to what extent had we lost, in terms of ancient controls, the old freedoms, the right and ability to challenge, our control on labour, loyalty to the Union? To have lost completely would have meant all of these things had gone, and we'd crawled back to work defeated grateful to have a job at any price. Much in fact like the hapless souls in Germinal. In 1992 I set off to find out taking as examples collieries from Scotland through England and Wales where it was know different types of strategy were being deployed, basically hard cop soft cop. In depth I looked at Maltby, Hatfield Main, in Yorkshire and Ellington and Easington in the Northumbria coalfield, all of whom had fairly local contracts of the new type aimed at driving out the union; Thorsby in Notts, which operated a traditional contact system with a modern overlay addition on top; the traditional area incentive schemes negotiated by area Unions and guided by agreed national terms still applied in South Wales and Long-Gannet in Scotland. I was curious to what extent the new strategies affected the introduction of outside contractors, industrial relations behaviour, face manning, job control, cavilling and other forms of miners self deployment, the position of pit bonus earners as against that of face workers.

I discovered that all of the collieries with the exception of Wales, Scotland and Nottingham, which for different reason were having different styles of management applied to them, were at war in defence of job controls against management prerogatives. At Ellington in Northumberland the vast coal complex had been in protracted and bitter war against Management attempts to bring in outside contract workers and new contracts. This latter demanded fixed prices per strip of coal regardless of how few workers had to achieve it, therefore regardless of effort the reward remained the same and the target had to be met for payment. Strike ballots had been decisively won, and management had given back all major development work to the Unions own manning lists. The formal cavil system had been abolished with NPLA but face teams were self selecting and moved en block, management could not pick who went where. Face training and outbye job and therefore wage progression remained under the control of the lodge. No coal was allowed to be cut at the week-ends, and mid week overtime was allocated by the lodge, management request a certain number of bodies for week end work by Thursday evening at the latest, or none whatever are supplied, the lodge picks the workers on a rotor basis.

At Easington Colliery in Co. Durham, cavilling continued despite the existence of NPLA, face teams being self selecting, spare men filling in for regulars form the first full regular teams for new faces, the old regulars becoming spare, a method which infuriated management's with notions of team building and correct selection. Advanced pit contracts had been negotiated with substantial improvements in nationally agreed wage levels. The pit was at war over attempts to take back the contracts, and management were cutting back on time off work for union officials to do union work.

Maltby colliery in Yorkshire was at war, against determined efforts to break the pit from the Area Incentive Agreement having imposed a pit contract of 30,000 tonnes regardless of faces in production. Management justifying the extraordinary situation by insisting that this was the figure the pit required to break even and if it wasn't reached no bonus whatever would be paid. as at the other pits industrial relations went into steep decline together with production. The new scheme reduced outbye, i.e. non face earnings by 86% per week. The recent history of viscous industrial relations struggle had started in 1990 with the arbitrary withdrawal of the collieries own ambulance service. This was met by a series of rolling 24 hour strikes. Instead of the usual one day per week on strike, the action was spread over the whole week, Wednesday day shift struck, Thursday afters shift struck, Friday night shift struck. It proved massively disruptive. It was followed by go slows, rag-ups and a climate of sullen hostility.

The origin of the modern mining contract and more particularly the motivation for its introduction is a story too long in the telling for this book. Suffice it to say, the National Power Loading Agreement, was a landmark in mining industrial relations, it had levelled all workers nationwide, so that the face man in Scotland would earn the same as the face man in Kent, the same job paid the same rate. It also massively focused attention on national pay bargaining since everyone wages depended on the outcome the strength of the Unions argument and their bargaining power. Twice in as many years miners pay demands would rock the Tory government and finally in 74 led to its collapse. Those who would rule the country, Labour and Tory dreamed up ways back then of first disarming or weakening the miners and then of smashing them, far sighted reactionary visionaries dreamed of getting rid of the miners altogether, though the time for that argument had not yet come, and it was the Labour government who introduced against the expressed wishes of the membership the Area incentive schemes aimed at dividing the workers and ending national pay bargaining and therefore the standing of the union. However soon the view was being expressed that the NUM was too powerful and dominated the working of the schemes NCB strategists complained it had been subverted. The Monopolies and Mergers Commission report into the coal industry reported "in one week in 1982 over 50% of all faces and 75% of all drivages were achieving above 105% performance. The top 25% of faces were achieving 120% with the best 25% of drivages topping 140%. The fact that faces and drivages were regularly achieving performances of 130% and 140% demonstrated that that the Union at local level had gained control over the scheme itself" (NUM internal doc). The report had detailed how incentive earning levels were "... far above what may be attributed to human effort in relation to normal work study standards".

The Area scheme as far as Coal Board and Government strategists was still too centralised, too regulated by appeals through conciliation machinery and the structure of the NUM. The post strike situation with an exhausted adversary already all but derecognised at national level with areas in disarray and real poverty following the 12 months without wages for workers at pit level, the way seemed open to impose a new form of contract. Chief target was Doncaster, Ray Richardson and Stephen Wood in the British Journal of Industrial Relations tell us "From what we were told it is quite clear that management in the old Doncaster Area consciously designated new industrial relations strategy during the strike and were poised to implement it when the strike finished." Chief among their goals was to "reduce the power of the NUM over all aspects of pit life," a further stated aim, and one I might add which is timeless in the mining industry was "reassert managerial prerogative".

Whilst the previous Area incentive scheme had attracted meticulous attention to the recording of delays, the Doncaster Option invited the whole workforce to collaborate in their elimination. Under the new scheme no delays would be paid, but running time would be paid at double the standard of the old rate. Chargemen and Union officials changed overnight from identifying delays outwith the control of the men and thus attracting payment, to pouring over reams of delay analysis sheets together with management in order to target production blockages and improve coal clearances.

The first thing I discovered when reviewing bonus earnings following the introduction of the new scheme in Doncaster was that pit earnings were running at 2/3rds those of the face earnings, almost an exact recreation of the balance that existed before, and the strength of pit Union branches ensured that the level would be held there.

Richardson and Wood believed that the new scheme had been custom built to break down solidarity and undercut the power of the NUM. If that had been so, it undoubtedly failed, firstly real earnings rose for all workers, although more rapidly for the face men. In addition came a management contradiction, as tonnage's started to rise, the need to keep the tram on the rails forced them to back off more contentious inroads into Union power. The Doncaster pits were holding tight to their priority systems. Two of the major post-85 strikes centred on the Doncaster coalfield, at Bentley and then at Hatfield Collieries where management deemed they had the right to remove workers from strategic developments if they felt their work "unsatisfactory" and place them on less important work. Our priority systems said we deployed the men and struck, eventually picketing out two whole coalfields until the management conceded defeat. Reluctantly as disputes arose over the Doncaster option the Area apparatus of the Union who had hated the new scheme were forced to become involved in conciliation and negotiation over its terms, the direction of control shifted from Doncaster to the Area Coal Board apparatus, the scheme on all counts had been subverted too with precious little gained as far as reasserting managerial prerogatives were concerned.

Next they shifted the goal posts from the coalfield, to the pit and opened the way for the introduction of *colliery* incentive and bonus schemes, the idea was to wheel barrow loads of money to key groups of workers, circumvent the Union apparatus and screw Down payments to non producers. Firm discipline among the miners however rejected any talk on any subject with management unless the Union had set the ground rules and negotiations were with the branch officers, no contracts would be agreed without the wholehearted support of the entire colliery workforce. This led to a dramatic escalation of industrial warfare, the colliery rarely being at peace or for long at work, while negotiations frequently gave way to physical violence between Union and Management and the calm air of Cooper and Lybrands lunch time communications were rent asunder by tea cups bouncing off the table, phones being ripped out of walls and thrown through windows and actual fights breaking out in the pit yard as management came face to face to Union officials. It was to end with the most furious strike, with court injunctions, threats of imprisonment, pickets wearing ski masks to avoid detection, and an escalating sum of damages laid against us as the pickets defied all laws and brought out the coalfields.

Finally when we had reached the eleventh hour of the writs and we were on the verge of bankruptcy and having our houses possessed, we very publicly before a mass meeting of the men and the cameras agreed to call off the pickets, and the men pledged to do so, pit head cameras mounted to detect breaches of the order were astonished to find the pits continuing to come up and the strike continuing to spread, and not a picket in sight. "How are they doing it" the Area Director was screaming as more and more collieries came out "they've stopped picketing but pits are still coming out!" Well Mr Houghton the Area Director didn't know that this was the age of the phone, a few phone calls to key activists at one pit after another, ensured that as men gathered in the canteens prior to descending the mine, up one would get, announcing: "The Hatfield pickets won't be here tonight; the courts have threatened to declare the Union officials bankrupt and send in the bailiffs for damages costs, and if that fails they will be jailed. I know if the Hatfield pickets had come I would have went home. "So would we," came the response. "Then what are we waiting for?" Off they would all go, and so it spread. Let your fingers do the walking, as the phone company said.

The result was a stormy industrial relations meeting with no holds barred, and a bursting of the contract logjam. We got Union negotiations and opened up whole areas to incentive payments who had previously suffered disproportionately to the face men. Now all groups could have financial incentives. This wasn't quite what the Company strategist had in mind. Now it was the National Wage rates which they had set that were undermined in favour of the men. At my colliery, material workers had an enhanced income of £97.45 per week without overtime, pit bottom workers £75.30 and surface banksmen, always previously the poor relations, were receiving never less than £71 per week more than they had done, without overtime. Branch meetings, discussing as they did contracts, big sums of money and terms of work, were never more popular and massive. The Union had, it seemed, worked the oracle again. Branches like Hatfield imposed a minimum standard of 2/3rds of the average face bonuses for 100% pit bonus earners, exactly the same ratio as had operated under the Area incentive scheme, and had been held to under the Doncaster Option scheme, with the added attraction that the gross figures were anyway vastly improved.

It was around this time, that I believe someone among the powers that be looked at the trajectory of resistance and independence and strength of Union control, still overwhelmingly present in the pits *after* the defeat of '85, and all the clever contracts schemes developed in covert government think tanks afterwards, and concluded that this bird's political wings could never be effectively clipped; we should have to be decisively culled. This strategic group of workers, still the supplier of more than 85% of all power generation, was to get rid of the industry as the major supplier of power. The opportunity presented itself in terms of the privatisation of the power generation utilities. No longer would they be obliged to burn the cheapest fuel, they could take it from where they wanted, abroad, or else move into the get-rich-quick gas generators being giving the go ahead by the government. Nuclear power would be cranked up regardless of cost from a base supply of less than 10% to 30% despite its 130% excess cost of coal-generated power. In Scotland, Scottish Nuclear would move into _chief_ supply position for the energy market. Coals market vanished overnight, with the market would go the pits and those troublesome miners who had plagued the lives of the ruling class for so long. It would not be too fanciful, I think, to say that the mining communities' refusal and point blank rejection of all the mores supposedly imposed by the regime of the industrial revolution - facelessness, discipline, respect for authority, subservience etc. - something which had bedevilled the ruling class for centuries when our labour and our mineral was indispensable, now conspired as motive enough for our final elimination, now that the world was awash with surplus energy sources.

There is perhaps not time to tell the tale of our last great stand in '93. Suffice to say some 19,257 British Coal miners voted to strike, while 16,734 outside contract miners voted likewise. Joint action with railworkers and many taking sympathetic action resulted in 12 million lost workdays on just two days of strike action and despite the movement by literally millions of people to stop the last savage swathes of closure we lost. Of British Coals 187,000 miners who struck in '84, only 8,000 miners remain in the whole industry. British Coal is no more, in a final coup de grace the industry was sold off to two major and a number of minor coal companies, death and injury rates are rising, the whip hand of the sack and the prospect of the dole queue, together with the blacklist ensures that now only something like 60% of miners belong to the Union, in 1996 they voted by 80% to strike again but were thwarted by legal action and the courts. In March '99 they again voted for all out unlimited strike action by 57% despite ever falling numbers, actually succeeded in squeezing Union recognition from the coal owners and a greatly increased pay award.

However the frontier is being pushed back nationwide only 33% of workers belong to Unions the lowest in 50 years despite the microprocessor revolution, capitalism in the 1990s is return-ing to a more exploitative form. A decade and a half of free market Thatcherism has repro-duced levels of relative social inequality unseen since Victorian times, continuing mass un-employment the virtual destruction of manufacturing industry, the impoverishment of the traditional proletarian areas, a social infrastructure in terminal decline. A rise in anti-social crime, relentless destruction of health, education, pensions and welfare. Yet throughout the period, bank clerks and schoolteachers, civil servants and railworkers, dockers and under-ground rail workers continue to strike and resist new work patterns, individual contracts and attacks upon collective identity and struggle. On the other hand at the same time we see widespread revolt at the apparent achievements of progress, determined resistance to motor-way and road construction, mass blockades and attacks upon machinery in defence of na-ture. Massive and sustained objection to animal exports and the slaughter industry which have paralysed ports and airports and brought young and old, working class and middle class protesters into violent confrontation with the defenders of the free flow of the market. In the '60s a good proportion of my generation living in the midst of relative affluence and potential gross consumerism, stepped back and rejected it, turning instead to struggles for individual liberty, class justice, an end to sexism and racialism, an exploration of mysticism and free sexuality. Today there are strong surges of that same stiff breeze blowing across the world as young people turn to new ageism and renewed interest in Anarchism and respect for the planet and its diverse peoples; is consumerism and abundance of wealth and property still heady as it was a decade ago?

The industrial revolution, its impact and morality, its old obstacles and conflicts, are still running their course. Perhaps it's too early to judge the outcome but nowt is settled yet. In part it's down to THIS generation, or, as the old man once said, "The point is, to change it".

Footnote

Specific facts referred to in this discourse come from my earlier *Coal Communities in Con-flict*, Published by Class War, and *Pit Life In County Durham*, published by The History Workshop, Oxford, as well as:
Northumberland and Durham, a social and political miscellany, Frank Graham.
The Colliers Rant, Robert Coll, Pub Rowman and Littlefield.
The Miners Association, Trade Union in the Age of The Chartists, Raymond Challinor and Brian Ripley.
The Class Struggle in 19th Century Oxfordshire, Bernard Reaney, pub History Workshop, Oxford.
Dark Tales of Old Newcastle, Pamela Armstrong, Pub Bridge Studios, Northumberland.

Broadly, all these have been used in the preparation of lectures and seminars to students at Wellesley College, Mass. USA, who did me the honour of inviting me to talk in '95 & '96 as part of their studies on Class and Resistance.

THIS IS CLASS WAR

The Class War Federation is an organisation of groups and individuals who have come together to change the Society we live in, to improve the lot of working class people.

This Society is divided into classes based on control of its institutions and wealth. The Ruling Class - those who "own" the factories or natural resources - whether it's through shares or being chairman of the board etc., who are under normal circumstances supported by the Middle Class - those who gain their position in society by patronage of the Ruling Class - who carry out their dirty work of controlling and (dis)organising the working class who do all the necessary work. Such a society is the root cause of most of the problems experienced by Working Class people the World over. as the Ruling Class has every intention of keeping its privileged position it must be destroyed- this is Class War.

Real change can only come about by working class people organising themselves to deal with the problems that they experience and to provide for ourselves. It is not about becoming better treated slaves but masters of our destiny. Direct action is necessary against the individuals and institutions who stand in the way of this. There is no alternative. Violence is a necessary part of the Class War - not as elitist terrorists but as an integrated part of the Class - they started it, we'll have to finish it!

Class society creates other abuses based upon the prejudices of Ruling or Middle Class such as gender, ethnic origin, sexuality, disability. The Ruling Class often use these to divide our class. We must unite on the basis of we have in common our Working Class backgrounds and needs.

The Class must fight these divisions, on all fronts. Above all the CWF believes that politics cannot be separated from life - and life from politics. We reject the missionary/ righteous so called "revolutionary" Left. Our politics must be fulfilling and relevant to our every day lives.

Working Class people must take responsibility for their progressive revolutionary politics - fly by night middle class radicals have been the bane of our movement for as long as the Working Class has existed.

OUR AIM

Therefore the aim of the CWF is to increase the militancy and self awareness of the Working Class in defending their interests and solving their problems. We do this through propaganda, active participation and debate as equals.

Appendix 3
Things That Go Bump!

A two and a half page precis of 28 pages of "outrages"contained in
a secret report compiled by "The National Working Miners Committee"
(the blackleg organisation set up by the state) and presented to parliament
in support of "tougher measures" against the miners

The scale of the "Hit Squad" activity is undeniable, or if anything under-rated, however some
of the detail is faulty, particularly where they have simply scanned the national papers, and
reprinted any stories they thought would be useful.

So it was that the National Working Miners Committee, the scab outfit established in conjunction with the government to break the strike complied a list of outrages committed by the
striking miners in the first five months of the 1984 strike. This was presented to special
parliamentary bodies established to meet the challenge of the strike. Unlike the desperate and
disposed of Germinal who raid the countryside in starvation, we did not think ourselves
desperate, neither where we starving, we knew only that we were angry and determined, and
I suppose on reflection, invincible. We have reprinted here a rapid random selection of
'outrages'. The full glorious chronicle of resistance is available from Hatfield Main Branch of
the NUM or Class War on request.

PERSONS

March 13. 300 flying pickets from Yorkshire force the closure of a Nottingham pit after fights
and scuffles.

March 15. Solitary strike breaker agrees to stop scabbing after facing pickets and finding his
car overturned with a lump of concrete through the windscreen.

March 24. At hem heath, strike breakers found their windscreens smashed tyres ripped and
concrete and metal objects strewn in the roads "Pickets had urinated into plastic bags and
thrown them at men going to work".

March 26. Young miner Ian Tarren hangs himself after being discovered working.

April 5. Violence at Silverdale Colliery pickets attacked cars transporting strike breakers.

April 19. Strike breakers punched and car windows smashed at Hem heath.

May 4. 18 pickets arrested for stoning strike breakers at Cotgrave Colliery.

May 12. Chunks of metal sawn from steel rods catapulted at strike breakers at Rufford Colliery.

May 18. 3 Yorkshire miners arrested for attacks upon Nottingham strike breakers charged
with conspiracy.

June 27. Windows of buses and cars smashed following ambush by strikers at Shirebrook.
Seven arrests, two police officers injured.

June 21. James Clay committed suicide after pressure for working.

July 27. 52 arrests after 300 pickets tore down fencing and started bonfires at Bilston Glen, 40
arrests after strikers surround home of strike breakers.

August 8. Birch Coppice Colliery in Warwickshire coaches attacked.

Cumbria 23 north eastern pickets detained after lorry drivers attacked and injured at the coal

loading station at Maryport, drivers taken to hospital, criminal damage.
Brake pipes of a car belonging to strike breaker from Hucknall Colliery severed.
Bricks and paint hurled at deputies reporting for work.
Aug. 9. Harworth Colliery, 1000 pickets attacked strike breakers turning up for work on the Afternoon shift (I ended up digging one of their gardens but that's another story).
Strike breaker attacked in wine bar Staffordshire (beats doing it at 4 am at the pit gates).
Aug. 10. Monty Morgan 54 went to work at Garw Colliery South Wales he was pelted with eggs bricks and bottles by over 300 strikers, their wives and children. Seven arrests were made and it was three hours after the end of the shift before he could get away from the pit. Nottingham Area of the NCB report £150,000 worth of criminal damage.In addition £40,000 worth of damage to 422 vehicles.
Aug. 11. £3,000 sports car owned by a strike breaker destroyed in an arson attack.
Aug. 21. Fred Cantrell Thurcroft strike breaker bricks thrown through his windows.
Aug. 23. 5 Instances of windows being broken in strike breakers homes in Derbyshire strike breaker on way to work at Shirebrook Colliery had his car attacked by iron bar wielding picket.
Aug. 29. A cable strung at neck height across a road, strike breaker miner hit the cable and was catapulted off his motorbike (someone knew the old song!).
Aug. 30. 87 strikers arrested in Scotland as strikers surround home of strike breaker.
Aug. 31. 3 men arrested after petrol bomb attack on car of strike breaker.
Petrol bombs thrown at car exploded but caused slight damage.
Sept. 6. 12 miners from north Derbyshire charged with riot in connection with attack on strike breakers.
Maintenance workers at Betteshanger Kent attacked and injured as he emerged from pit.
Sept. 28. Staffordshire NUM official charged with attacking strike breaker and damaging his car.
Sept. 22. 2500 pickets at Shirebrook Colliery bricks thrown hay bales set alight and attempts to push police under vehicles.
John Roberts from Markham said his car had been stoned, oil poured on his road and ball bearings fired at his window, another vehicle had swerved in a deliberate attempt to overturn his car.
Sept. 29. Striking miner who set fire to a coach being used to carry strike breakers in Lancashire sentenced to nine month.
POLICE
Oct. 2. Bob Taylor Manton Strike breaker run off road by strikers.
March 15. 7 Police Officers hurt at Ollerton Colliery, 300 pickets block main gate, strike breakers were punched and police pelted with bricks, lumps of wood, milk bottles and fireworks.
March 24. 800 pickets at Cadley Hill Colliery South Derbyshire police injured and 3 police coaches damaged.
March 28. Doncaster pickets charged with Breach of the peace, assault and criminal damage in fighting outside NCB Headquarters..
March 29. Police Officer dragged along in a car during a blockade of the M1. Motorway.
April 4. Pickets violently attack police outside Port Talbort steelworks South Wales.
April 6. 39 arrests as 350 Nottingham and Northumbrian miners picket at Port Talbot steelworks.
April 11. police find 4 inch nails welded into weapons at Silverdale Colliery picket.
April 13. lead filled bottle cap with four screws sticking out thrown at police lines, police injured.

April 19. Police injured at Wivenhoe Docks.

May 2. Stones thrown and arrests made on A38 as police mount blockade. County Durham police officer receives broken arm during fighting at Inkerman open cast mine, another hit on head by missile thrown at Lumley Thicks open cast.

May 5. 19 arrests and police injured as 2000 miners siege Hucknall Colliery.

May 9. Two officers hurt, five arrests at Pye Colliery Nottingham as 2500 pickets besiege pit.

May 10. Hall used by police Burnt down at Gedling Colliery. At Creswell criminal damage public disorder and assaults on police 20 officers hurt 13 arrests.

May 11. Silverdale Colliery 30 arrests as police suffer barrages of stones.

May 12. nails hammered into wood and concealed in paper bags and cigarette packets and strewn on roads in effort to maim police horses.

May 15. 55 men in court charged with riot after mass rally in Mansfield, 88 arrests made and 40 police hurt in fighting.

May 22. Police hurt when concrete block thrown through window of police van near Rufford Colliery.

May 25. 45 arrests after 5 strike breakers tried to pass through 150 pickets & fighting erupts with police.

May 30. 84 arrested and 64 injured at Orgreave. Stones wooden fencing thrown at police who were also bombarded with smoke bombs and firecrackers, one officer sustained a broken leg.

May 31. Orgreave Miners left a telegraph pole a battering ram barbed wire and a burning portacabin across the road to halt police charges. 15 arrests 16 police injured plus a horse.

June 7. 23 arrests eight police injured three burnt with paintstripper.

June 18. Maltby Colliery 29 arrests police injured one with broken nose.

June 19. At Orgreave 80 were injured 100 arrests following horrifying scenes, stones bottles bricks iron bars and jagged glass thrown at police. Barricades of burning cars, lamp posts and stones from a wall they had demolished. Wooden stakes to halt police horses planted in ground.

June 20. 20 charged with riot at Orgreave.

July 3. Five offices injured in fighting at Shirebrook Colliery.

July 7. Selby, violent encounters as pickets occupy toll bridge.
Police vehicles overturned at Whitemore mine.

July 11. Stones thrown and windows broken at Hemsworth police station, police raid nearby pub The Fitzwilliam and are avalanched by stones and bottles.

Aug. 14. Three miles from Welbeck Colliery 2000 pickets clash with police at road blocks, bricks and stones hurled at police, officers injured.

Aug. 17. Gascoigne Wood policeman had nose broken pickets set fire to rolls of straw dragged from nearby fields and into approach road, police coaches stones, shattered windows and knocked police motorcyclist from his vehicle.

Aug. 18. Fighting at Gascoigne Wood, bricks hurled at police, Selston nr Mansfield police car stoned and windows broken.

Aug. 22. Silverwood Colliery 1000 pickets massed before dawn to prevent a solitary strike breaker going in, they burnt scrap cars, trees and supermarket trolleys in the road and launched a barrage of bricks and stones at police, eight officers hurt.
Ugly scenes at Hatfield where pickets set up barricades of trees and set an old car on fire on a road to close the colliery. Police car had its windows smashed by stones in a neighbouring

village.

Aug. 23. Senior police offices admitted that they were deeply concerned at the emergence of a paramilitary style gang apparently led by a women which spearheaded a day Of unprecedented violence in Yorkshire pit villages. They were dressed in camouflage jackets boiler suites and balaclava helmets.

Police fought pickets in villages surrounding the pits of Bentley, Markham Main and Yorkshire Main after barricades were erected and set on fire, pit stores looted and equipment wrecked. At Bentley 50 people led by a women were spotted, uniformed in the pit yard.They attacked spy cameras and stole donkey jackets and pickaxe handles.

Aug. 24. Forensic scientists examined three suspected petrol bombs found by police after they clashed with pickets They were discovered in a garden after running battles outside Markham colliery.

Sept. 1. Police horse stoned to the ground and injured 3 officers had glass shattered in their eyes when their coach was attacked in the worst violence so far at Kiverton Park Colliery, South Yorkshire. Windscreens were shattered together with two large windows of a metropolitan police coach as it was pelted with rocks.

Sept. 7. 13 hurt in fighting at Kellingley Colliery were 4000 pickets gathered. Police showered with broken glass and pieces of concrete outside the pit, where two strike breakers had gone in. A News van was overturned and set on fire.

Sept. 11. An array of weapons used by miners pickets were put on show by police included were a heavy chain, ball bearings and booby traps designed to maim men, horses and dogs. Two pickets who covered the road with spiked belts to stop police bringing in blacklegs at Dunfermline were sentenced.

PROPERTY

March 15. Ollerton Colliery, lorry windows smashed, head injuries.

March 27. Women Coal Board clerks knocked down and others were kicked and spat on when 200 marauding pickets swamped a force of thirty police on guard outside NCB's Doncaster HQ.

May 2. 17 arrests outside Littleton Colliery, coach windows smashed Trentham Workshops attacked with a crowbar.

May 8. 23 arrests Hunterston Coal Depot, three lorries windshields smashed.

May 10. Coach taking clerks to Duckmanton Derbyshire NCB HQ attacked with bricks and stones, windows smashed several strike breakers injured. Damage at Oxcroft where 11000 volt electric cable carrying the main power supply is severed, office windows broken.

Pleasey Colliery, 6 heavy plant vehicles destroyed and sand poured into petrol tanks, Windows smashed in all buildings and the pit closed due to sabotage.

Langwith Colliery where only surface work continues surface vehicles set on fire.

May 11. Duckmanton, coach of 20 strike-breaker clerks stopped and stoned and occupants injured Sherwood Colliery two belts carrying slag from the pit head slashed.

June 7. Pit top conveyor belts cut through at Silverdale Colliery. Damage of £10,000 caused to machinery and telephone lines at private open cast mine in Lanarkshire.

June 27. 37 strike breaking clerks at Doncaster's regional HQ assaulted, hit by stones and otherwise threatened.

July 6. Clerical staff at Shirebrook Colliery stoned and abused.

July 10. 13 terrified NCB managers and maintenance staff rescued by police after being held under siege for 11 hours, while windows were smashed and property damaged. Four more South Wales haulage firms conveying coal and iron ore supplies to Llanwern have been attacked, 13 lorries have been damaged, paint sprayed on windshields and sugar poured into fuel tanks.

July 11. £100,000 damages done to drift mine near Llanwern and many vehicles set on fire. Port Talbot 500 pickets smashed lorry windows, 34 arrests including 7 women.

July 21. 6 articulated lorries which had been moving coal from Nottingham pits to power stations set ablaze £200,000 worth of damage. Three other lorries owned by another company also attacked.

Aug. 4. 200 miners vandalised NCB transport depot in Derbyshire, 14 lorries and 2 coaches attacked.

Aug. 7. 10 coal hauling vehicles attacked.

Aug. 8. 60 men stoned NCB offices in Doncaster, many windows smashed.

Aug. 9. 5 Northumbrian miners sentenced for an attack on a fleet of lorries using pick axe handles and sledge hammers.

95 arrests in Nottingham as busses stoned.

Private open cast mine at Westerhope Newcastle Upon Tyne, sabotaged.

Aug. 13. Five coaches belonging to the NCB were destroyed after flammable material thrown over them, the office block was also attacked causing £30,000 worth of damage.

Aug. 17. 25 year old miner in court, charged with the destruction by fire of 3 coaches and a van at Trentham Colliery.

Aug. 21. 6 Hem Health strikers remanded in custody for burning two coaches.

A striking North Derbyshire miner who carried out a sabotage attack upon NCB Depot jailed for nine months.

Aug. 13. County Durham taxi firm used by NCB to take in strike breakers, offices and telephones
attacked and vehicles vandalised.

Aug. 25. Riot, Easington Colliery, office staff forced to shelter in corridors as bricks smashed windows, and 500 pickets rampaged through the colliery car park cars were damaged including that of the colliery manager, an Audi was overturned, police officers injured.

Sept. 11. 35 men in court at Chesterfield charged with Unlawful assembly after £1000's worth of damage to NCB vehicles and police cars.

Sept. 20. Frank Allen and his son Kevin charged with threatening behaviour possessing pickaxe handles and attempting to beset a place of employment, namely Bolsover Colliery.

Sept. 26. Pickets in South Wales ambush 140 strong convoy of heavy lorries ferrying coal and iron ore along the M4 from Port Talbot to Llanwern Steelworks. 10 vehicles damaged, police produce a 4 ft wooden pit prop as one of the missiles hurled, windscreens smashed and large stone crashed through one lorries glass fibre roof.

And so it continued, eventually costing 8 lives, 12,000 arrests, 800 serious injuries, lengthy jail terms including two life sentences 1,000 sackings and blacklistings, evictions, bankruptcies, divorces, and to the state the estimate is around £12 billion, more than was spent in the whole Falklands War adventure. But the truth is they hadn't, despite all that, decisively WON, not at this time. The NUM was *still* there, still combative, and still capable of blowing on the embers of the fire, and restarting the rebellion.